EVIDENCE
for JESUS

RALPH O. MUNCASTER

HARVEST HOUSE PUBLISHERS

EUGENE, OREGON

Cover by Dugan Design Group, Bloomington, Minnesota

Jars photo on cover © Jeff Greenberg / Index Stock Imagery / PictureQuest

EVIDENCE FOR JESUS
Copyright © 2004 by Ralph O. Muncaster
Published by Harvest House Publishers
Eugene, Oregon 97402
www.harvesthousepublishers.com

Library of Congress Cataloging-in-Publication Data
Ralph O. Muncaster
  Evidence for Jesus / Ralph O. Muncaster
        p. cm.
Includes bibliographical references
  ISBN 978-0-7369-1275-4
  1. Jesus Christ—Historicity. 2. Apologetics I. Title.
  BT303.2.M86   2004
  232.9'08—dc22   2003015553

Printed in the United States of America

17 18 19 20 / VP-CF / 15 14 13 12 11

Contents

Why Test the Bible's Claims About Jesus?

Dawn was breaking over the lush tropical forest. Mothers were cuddling babies who were crying as they awaited their morning milk. Young children were already gleefully running to find friends to join them in their early morning games. And fathers struggled to roll out of bed to begin the day's arduous schedule of work in the fields. It seemed like any other day.

Daily routine required working in the fields from 7 A.M. to 6 P.M. with an hour break for lunch. The almost constant preaching over loudspeakers by the group's exalted leader filled the dense jungle air. Daily toil and suffering was thought of as holy, something that was admired. The commitment to hard work reflected the extent of commitment to their leader and God. During the day, news was quickly spreading that this night might be the great "white night" that everyone was waiting for—when they would achieve their ultimate spiritual awakening for the glory of their cause. People looked forward to having a chance to bring honor to themselves, glory to their beliefs, and to achieve eternal utopia.

That evening the standard drill began. "Blaaam! Assemble! Crash!" Sounds echoed through the camp as 50 armed guards scrambled about, bursting through the doors of each cabin telling people to assemble because their lives were in danger. Shouts rang. Running. Excitement. The crowd murmured in anticipation as they bustled to the meeting area. The leader, standing over six feet tall, lean and strong, had a face revealing a suspicious air of tenderness and compassion for his people. His hair was coal black and his eyes seemed to pierce the very souls of all glued to his every word.

"Today is the day," he said in a rich, deep voice.

Everyone knew what he meant and knew what to do. They'd rehearsed it so many times before. "Was this just another drill?" they thought. Families gathered together laughing, smiling, joyfully hugging each other and saying prayers for their future. Tears streamed down the faces of father and daughter alike. Then the families ran to stand in the line leading up to the altar where the leader stood; everyone was rushing to get there first.

One by one each person greeted the leader with a smile, then a hug, and received a drink, a concoction designed to help everyone know true peace and meet God—while bringing glory to their great cause. First the smallest children participated. Cute little toddlers of three or four. Young girls of six and seven. Youthful boys of ten and eleven. Teenagers. Young adults. And finally the mothers, fathers, and tiny babys—one by one, they all drank the special potion.

Next, the families retreated to private areas where they huddled in anticipation. Minutes passed. Then an eerie silence swept over the camp. The quiet seemed deafening. Within an hour, more than 900 people—from tiny babes to the elderly—were dead. People lay in horrifying heaps; piled one on top of the other—the ugly scene revealing each family's final moments as they clutched their loved ones and breathed their last breath. They were victims of poisoning by Kool-Aid laced with cyanide; 638 were adults and 276 were children. It was November 18, 1978. The place was Jonestown, Guyana. The exalted leader was Jim Jones.

LATE IN THE DAY THE PRISONERS WERE GATHERED together in a crude outdoor arena. They were of all ages and backgrounds. Some were only teenagers, including young girls with innocent beauty, intelligence, and a promising future. There were also strong, virile, young boys with years of hope and joy ahead of them. Others in the crowd included expectant mothers, fathers, merchants, teachers, and laborers. The group was filled with anxiety, and each person secretly knew that nothing good could come from such a gathering.

A Roman centurion stood on a makeshift platform to address the crowd.

"People of Rome, your great Emperor Trajan has declared your God an enemy to our empire. He demands your loyalty and honor in receiving himself as god, the one you should worship, as the rest of our land does. In that regard, you must renounce your leader—or as you claim, your "God"—and bow down to a statue of Trajan in reverence and worship to him, or you will be put to death."

A young wife, Martha, who was expecting her first child, looked up at her husband with tears in her eyes. "What do we do?" she cried.

Joshua, her husband, stared straight ahead to avoid the pain of seeing the fear in his wife's eyes. He steadied his voice as best as possible, and replied, "The Master told us this day would come.

He said we would be asked to make a sacrifice of ourselves for his sake. Our actions in a time like this reflect our sincerity and our commitment to him. How can we let him down now?"

"So you mean we must give up our entire future, our entire lives together, and our unborn child's life to satisfy him? Couldn't we just go along with Trajan's request for a while and return to the Master's teaching later on?" Martha asked.

"No," Joshua sternly responded. "It just wouldn't be right. We can't deny him after what he did for us. And besides, he told us this would happen, and that if we remain strong, we are assured of a special place in heaven."

With that, Martha and Joshua proceeded forward in the line along with the others. When they reached the front Martha looked up at the face of the centurion, hardened with seemingly cast-iron wrinkles from years of executing hundreds of people with merciless punishment. He stared harshly down at Martha cowering below him and asked the fateful question. Would she renounce her master and pledge allegiance to Trajan? Would she bow down and worship Trajan as her new god?

Martha paused for a moment as she pondered one of the most important decisions of her entire life. She looked over at Joshua, who was being asked the same questions simultaneously by another centurion. Joshua looked back at her. They were both thinking the same thoughts at the same time. Martha burst out sobbing, with tears flowing profusely as she thought of her unborn child and what was about to happen. When her eyes met Joshua's she knew exactly what she must do.

"No," they both answered. Their fate was sealed.

The two were solemnly taken away to a place where others ahead of them were already gathered. They were bound tightly to two posts. A special wax was poured over them, soaking into their clothing and covering every pore of their exposed skin. Then the soldiers appeared carrying torches. Martha looked over at Joshua, bound to his stake, semifrozen in hardened wax. Their eyes met. It was bittersweet. Both felt overwhelming sadness for life in the present, yet had joyful anticipation for eternal life. The torch touched the wax on Martha, and immediately she burst into flame. Then it was Joshua's turn.

As scarlet ribbons of fire streaked to the heavens, so did the spirits of Martha and Joshua. The place was Rome. The date was November 18, 124. Their master was Jesus Christ.

Jim Jones or Jesus Christ? In each case the people felt strongly about their leader before they met their deaths. How do we really know who was right? As the Jim Jones example pointed out, there are many documented cases where a leader gained the confidence of others and eventually wooed them into an untimely death. Recent examples include David Koresh in Waco, Texas, and Marshall Applewhite, who deluded Heaven's Gate followers in San Diego, California. These leaders, however, are extreme and rare. Perhaps though, even more dangerous are the leaders who woo far more people into a religion that is really false by making such wonderful promises that people follow them and reject the one true way. These types of leaders are commonplace. And such leaders seem far more acceptable than the extreme ones. But isn't the end result—luring people into a false hope that ends in eternal death—just as deadly? Their ability to attract much larger crowds than the extreme leaders makes them far more dangerous.

Selection of Jesus Christ as a leader is serious. He said we must follow him and reject the false teaching of others. Like the early Christians, for some people in certain countries, following Jesus is a potential life or death decision. For most people today, however, it is not a fatal decision for life on earth. However, according to Jesus, in all situations following him or not has consequences regarding eternal life. The options are simply stated: Follow him and have eternal life; reject him and don't have eternal life.

> Whoever believes in the Son has eternal life, but whoever rejects the Son will not see life, for God's wrath remains on him (John 3:36).

So the decision to follow Jesus is of enormous importance. And the decision to reject every other teaching is likewise of extreme importance. Many people rightfully ask, "How can we know that the Bible's teaching about Jesus is right?" "Aren't all religions basically the same?" Some people ask, "Why wouldn't God reveal himself in other holy books?" or, "Why wouldn't he reveal himself through other people as well?" "Why does Christianity have to be so narrow? It doesn't seem to make sense that such a big God would be 'boxed' into such a narrow religion as the Christianity taught by the Bible."

However, it doesn't matter what we "think" should be right. What really matters is *what is right,* whether it fits our personal view or not. *In that regard, we should consider what evidence is available to make an informed decision.*

Logical questions abound. People often wonder if the Bible really wants us to seek evidence regarding what it says or evidence about Jesus. What does the Bible say about this? Are we to simply accept its words on faith? The answer is no! The Bible commands us to "test everything," including the Bible itself:

> Test everything. Hold on to the good (1 Thessalonians 5:21).

Why would the Bible include such a command? Because untested faith is blind faith. And blind faith can lead to faith in anything. It can lead to faith in the religious leader of one's parents. It can lead to the most popular faith in the community. It can lead to the faith of friends. And it can even lead to faith in people such as Jim Jones, David Koresh, and Marshall Applewhite. However, *properly tested faith will only lead to the truth.* Therefore, if Jesus Christ is real and if the claims of the Bible regarding him are real, faith in him should be able to withstand being tested. People already having faith in the Bible would have nothing to fear. And if the Bible is wrong, shouldn't it be rejected anyway?

The following pages analyze the Jesus of the Bible. Was he real? Was he who he claimed to be—the long-awaited Messiah, the Son of God? Was he the salvation available to all mankind? For you who already believe in the Jesus of the Bible, this analysis will strengthen your faith. For you who question whether or not Jesus is real or whether he is who the Bible claims he is, this analysis will be revealing and life changing.

The Empty Tomb

RAYS OF SUNLIGHT STREAKED OVER THE GENTLY rolling hills on the east side of Jerusalem. It looked as if it would be a beautiful, sunny day. One by one people emerged from cozy stucco homes and strolled down the streets to their places of business. Rachel stopped at Rebecca's house hoping for companionship on her way to the well. Jacob ambled down to his carpenter shop to put the finishing touches on the latest new table set. And Achaeleus donned his armor before leaving for his shift at Herod's palace.

Outside the city gate what started as a whisper quickly rose to a roar throughout the city: "The body of Jesus, the teacher, has disappeared!"

The normally slow-moving city sprang quickly into fast-paced motion. Roman guards were running about the streets searching buildings, houses, and even the wooded areas surrounding the city. Where was the corpse of Jesus? An emergency session of the Sanhedrin was called by the religious leaders. How would they handle the public reaction to a "prophet" who predicted he would rise from the dead in three days? Many people roused family and friends from early morning activities. The news and gossip spread quickly. What had happened? Where did the body of Jesus go? Did he rise from the dead as he promised? Who saw him? Could it be that Jesus is really God?

WE CAN ONLY IMAGINE WHAT IT WAS LIKE in Jerusalem the day Jesus rose from the dead. Undoubtedly the news of the "missing" body was greeted differently depending on the perspective of each individual.

From the perspective of Herod, Pontius Pilate, and other Roman authorities, this introduced a new dilemma. Due to pressure from the local religious figures, they had acquiesced or agreed to the capital punishment of Jesus, despite unusual circumstances. Now they faced a potentially troublesome situation. How would the Pharisees and Sadducees maintain religious control if there was a groundswell of belief that Jesus rose from the dead? Jesus had prophesied his resurrection several times. His disciples were aware of it. The religious leaders were aware of it. And perhaps worst of all, part of the population of Jerusalem was aware of it. How would this news affect public opinion? Would people believe that Jesus truly overcame death? Would they believe that he was God? Would this cause volatile disputes between Jewish groups of people and disrupt Roman rule?

From the perspective of the Jewish religious leaders, it was a great disaster. They had presumed the execution of Jesus would eliminate his threat to their power once and for all. Now, Jesus' disciples might proclaim that he rose from the dead and was in fact God. If the disciples gained control of public opinion, they would further emphasize the teachings of Jesus, which had always undermined the power of the religious leaders. The very authority of the Jewish Council could be threatened. It could even mean the start of a new religion that could, perhaps, shake the foundations of centuries-old Judaism.

From the perspective of the people, there was confusion. The disciples were telling everyone that Jesus was seen after he died. What did this mean? Did Jesus really rise from the dead? Where was he? Exactly what did the disciples see? If Jesus really rose from the dead, did it verify his claim to be God? To many this might mean hope ... hope in the many things that Jesus taught during his life on earth. Hope of eternal life.

Original Concerns About the Corpse of Jesus

The Jewish leaders had obvious concerns about the corpse of Jesus from the outset. They realized that an unaccounted for body would cause tremendous problems and feared the potential public response if it should be found missing. So great was this concern, that they approached Pontius Pilate for a special favor as indicated in Matthew's gospel:

> The next day, the one after Preparation Day, the chief priests and the Pharisees went to Pilate. "Sir," they said, "we remember that while he was still alive that deceiver said, 'After three days I will rise again.' So give the order for the tomb to be made secure until the third day. Otherwise, his disciples may come and steal the body and tell the people that he has been raised from the dead. This last deception will be worse than the first" (Matthew 27:62-64).

This request brought the issue of Jesus' teachings back to Pilate's domain. Would Pilate's interest go beyond merely appeasing the Jewish leaders? Was he also concerned about the potential public impact if Jesus' corpse were to disappear? Did Pilate's concern reveal a deep-seated fear that Jesus might really be who he claimed to be? After all, that day Pilate's wife had warned him not to have anything to do with Jesus due to a premonition that she had:

> While Pilate was sitting on the judge's seat, his wife sent him this message: "Don't have anything to do with that innocent man, for I have suffered a great deal today in a dream because of him" (Matthew 27:19).

This message indicates that Pilate had been discussing Jesus in his private home with his wife. Jesus' status must have been of some particular interest prior to the night of the trial. Furthermore, Pilate seemed to do everything he could to set Jesus free, even to the extent of offering the criminal Barabbas as a "replacement." When the crowd insisted upon crucifying Jesus while Pilate was on the judgment seat, "[Pilate] washed his hands in front of the crowd. 'I am innocent of this man's blood,' he said. 'It is your responsibility'" (Matthew 27:24).

Whether Pilate's interest in monitoring the existence of Jesus' corpse was because of his fear of political problems or because of his curiosity or fear about Jesus' claims of deity, he quickly acquiesced to the high priest's requests to make the tomb secure: "'Take a guard,' Pilate answered. 'Go, make the tomb as secure as you know how.' So they went and made the tomb secure by putting a seal on the stone and posting the guard" (Matthew 27:65).

The Response of the Guard

The Roman guard (consisting of at least 16 soldiers) responsible for the tomb of Jesus was in obvious shock with the events of the resurrection. When they observed the angel who rolled away the stone covering the tomb, the Bible says they became "like dead men" (Matthew 28:4). The absence of Jesus' corpse presented them with a difficult problem. Typically, if such guards allowed a prisoner (or in this case a corpse) to escape while they were sleeping or deserting their posts, they would face the same sentence as the prisoner. In this case crucifixion. The guards were concerned for their fate resulting from the empty tomb because they first approached the religious leaders to obtain help in approaching the political authority, probably so the military leaders wouldn't punish them. In addition, there was a need to provide a cover-up for the disappearance of the corpse:

> Some of the guards went into the city and reported to the chief priests everything that had happened. When the chief priests had met with the elders and devised a plan, they gave the soldiers a large sum of money, telling them, "You are to say, 'His disciples came during the night and stole him away while we were asleep.' If this report gets to the governor, we will satisfy him and keep you out of trouble." So the soldiers took the money and did as they were instructed. And this story has been widely circulated among the Jews to this very day (Matthew 28:11-15).

So the Roman guard was essentially forced to provide a concocted story of sleeping while Jesus' disciples stole the body. In return for propagating the story, they received a large payment and protection from the highest local authority—the governor. But if they were sleeping, how would they know the disciples stole the body? They wouldn't have witnessed it. On the other hand, it would be difficult for 16 separate guards to keep the story of an angel with an appearance "like lightning" a secret for long (see Matthew 28:3). Someone would likely tell another person at some point in time. Just like today, when such a story "leaks" out, it eventually ends up in print—in the Bible in this case.

Nevertheless, the "official" story of the guards falling asleep and the disciples stealing the body was supported by the religious and political establishment, so it is easy to understand why it became the ongoing popular story among the Jews who opposed the Christians.

The Response of the Religious Leaders

The Jewish authorities had a serious problem. Jesus, who had prophesied that he would be raised from the dead in three days, was nowhere to be found three days after his crucifixion. It was their worst nightmare. Now the followers of Jesus could call him God and have evidence to back it up. It didn't take long for the effects of the resurrection to have a major impact. Jesus' disciples immediately started celebrating his deity and began promoting it throughout the region. Within days, thousands were following Jesus as the Savior of the world. The authority of the official Jewish leaders and their teachings started waning among many.

With no corpse to prove Jesus' human mortality, the authorities couldn't prove that Jesus was simply another human being. Since they desperately needed Jesus' corpse, the Jewish leaders would have certainly used every means at their disposal to hunt down and find it. Families, friends, acquaintances, and anyone who had known Jesus would have been questioned. Workers in the synagogues would have been enlisted to search the places where a body might have been placed. In short, if the body of Jesus could be found, Christianity would have been stopped dead in its tracks and the threat to historical Judaism would have ended. The Jewish authorities would maintain their rule. However, if the corpse could *not* be produced, the religious leaders' plight would be grave.

The Response of the Roman Leaders

The political establishment of Rome also had a stake in finding the corpse of Jesus. After all, Israel was a volatile religious state that could be threatened with any serious challenge to traditional Judaism. The teachings by Jesus were antiestablishment at their best and heretical revolutionary at their worst. However, they went even further when we consider that he positioned himself as God incarnate. Many Jews would be forced to deal with the complex and hard to understand issue of the Trinity, which states that God is three persons in one God (Jesus refers to this in Matthew 28:19).

So a conflict between the religious leaders and followers of Jesus seemed inevitable. It would clearly be in the best interest of the Roman establishment to find Jesus' corpse to keep the peace.

The Romans would have great resources at their disposal to attempt to find a body. Most importantly, they could invoke capital punishment on anyone found to be hiding the body. In fact, archaeology has located a first-century tomb in Nazareth that has an engraved message citing the death penalty for anyone found to be grave robbing. This unusual, harsh penalty, interestingly, was found in Jesus' hometown. It was placed at a grave site soon after the resurrection. Perhaps it was in response to it?

The Response of the Disciples

When we consider the disciples during the time of the crucifixion and resurrection, we realize it would be absurd to think they might have stolen the body of Jesus. First, we must consider the disciples' unstable state of mind. Even though they had been warned repeatedly by Jesus that he would be crucified and later raised from the dead, it was obvious they doubted the prophecy. On the critical night of the betrayal, the disciples didn't even stay awake. During the period of his trial, Peter denied him three times. When he was crucified, the disciples were scattered and there was reluctance to believe in the resurrection. In the case of Thomas, he stated he would believe only when he placed his hand into Jesus' wounds. None of these events are indicative of a band of well-organized disciples capable of quickly formulating a clever plan to steal a body under professional Roman guard.

Second, even if the disciples were motivated and ready to steal the body of Jesus, it would have been extremely difficult. The timing of the event would have occurred during the Sabbath (possibly even back-to-back Sabbaths since the day after Passover is always a "special Sabbath"—note John 19:31). Movement during the Sabbath was limited and would have been an obvious problem if the disciples were planning a major theft of a body. Then there was the issue of a ragtag band of disciples sneaking past the best trained guards in the world. Finally, there were the problems of moving a two-ton stone and breaking an official seal without detection.

The entire ministry of Jesus was focused on his role as the Son of God. In that role, the triumph over death through the resurrection was paramount. A dead Messiah would serve no purpose for the disciples. They had no motivation to steal the corpse of Jesus; it would be much simpler to just acknowledge they had been mistaken about Jesus. Furthermore, there would be nothing to gain by concocting a story of a resurrection and spreading it. To the contrary, once the persecution started, it would have been obvious that there was everything to lose by perpetuating a story of a phony messiah.

The Response of the Other Eyewitnesses

The twelve were not the only ones to see the risen Christ! For instance, we know that several women saw him on the day of the resurrection. There was Mary Magdalene, Salome, and "the other Mary" (possibly the wife of Clopas or the mother of James and Joses). We also know that Jesus appeared to many other people, including 500 people at one time (1 Corinthians 15:6).

Having so many other witnesses would make it more difficult for the religious leaders and Romans to sell the story of the disciples stealing the body. After all, why would other people, beyond the disciples themselves, claim to see the risen Christ?

Response of the City of Jerusalem

Jerusalem is faced with two opposing vantage points. On one side, the religious and political authorities indicated there was no corpse of Jesus because "against all odds" the disciples had stolen the body. Certainly these leaders would have commanded enormous respect from the populace. On the other hand, there were the disciples and other people who claimed to have witnessed the resurrection indicating that Jesus had risen and, hence, there would be no corpse. Of course, such a supernatural resurrection would also be against the odds. So the city had the dilemma of a difficult decision between their leaders and credible witnesses. At stake was a foundational change in religious belief. At stake were the lives of many.

The result of Jerusalem's decision to believe the leaders or the disciples immediately following the resurrection is historical. *The disciples and eyewitnesses won easily. Christianity exploded in the city, and within days, thousands of people became followers of Christ.* This is particularly significant because strict religious belief was of paramount importance to the Jews. The idea of a God that included Jesus as part of the Trinity was revolutionary. Yet by A.D. 70, some estimate that an enormous percentage of Jerusalem had become Christian. Even today, in a culture far more tolerant of diversity, it would be unheard of to envision a new religion taking over such a large part of the populace in such a short period of time. Yet we know Christianity grew very quickly. Otherwise there would have not been persecution that history records as occurring immediately. Christianity continued to spread in spite of the persecution.

Summary

In the days following the crucifixion, many precautions were taken to protect the corpse of Jesus, including the posting of a Roman guard. Even so, since the day of the resurrection, no body of Jesus has ever been located. There was every reason for the Jewish leaders to do everything they could in order to locate Jesus' body. Failure to do so would, and did, result in undermining their religious authority. Likewise, Roman leaders would have every incentive to do everything they could to locate the body of Jesus. Otherwise, a volatile dispute between the traditional Jews and followers of Jesus could ensue—and it did. This meant a threat to the peaceful Roman rule of Jerusalem and the surrounding territory.

It would have been virtually impossible for the haphazard band of disciples to overcome the Roman guard and steal the body of Jesus. Nor would there have been any reason for them to do so. Despite the explanation presented by the Jewish leaders and the Roman guards that the disciples had stolen the body, the city of Jerusalem was not accepting it. Instead, the people accepted the story presented by the eyewitnesses that Jesus had risen from the dead. Many gave their lives to verify this strong belief.

In a nutshell, all the Jewish leaders and Romans had to do in order to end Christianity forever was to produce the corpse of Jesus. They couldn't do it. And Christianity has since become the largest religion in the world.

The tomb was empty.

CONCLUSION

The inability of the Jewish leaders and the Romans to produce the corpse of Jesus is powerful evidence that it didn't exist—given that everything reasonable was done to protect it and there was no motivation for others to steal it. The logical conclusion would be that Jesus indeed rose from the dead.

High Security at the Tomb

C lang! Clang! Clang!" The hilts of metal swords beat a rhythm against the guards' body armor. Two boys hid behind the rock outcropping and watched as the soldiers marched with flair and precision only yards in front of them. "When I grow up I want to be a centurion," exclaimed young Titus.

"Me, too!" chimed Claudius, son of one of Pontius Pilate's administrators.

The boys watched as the guards strode up and took their positions in front of Jesus' tomb.

"It seems like such a waste of men just to guard a dead man," Titus said.

"Maybe," Claudius responded. "But didn't you hear the news? Jesus said he was going to rise from the dead in three days. If he does, they may need all 16 of those soldiers and a whole lot more!"

"Right!" Titus said sarcastically. "You don't really believe that, do you?"

"Of course not," said Claudius trying to sound confident and grown-up. "On the other hand, I wouldn't have believed he could've rescued ol' Lazarus from the dead either."

"You've got a point there," Titus conceded. With that the boys sat mesmerized, staring at the tomb of Jesus, each deep in thought about the body lying within and what mysteries might lay in store.

As THE PREVIOUS CHAPTER INDICATED, the Jewish religious leaders had a great concern about protecting the corpse of Jesus because they recognized that if the body were to disappear, it would be proclaimed a resurrection. Both the Pharisees and the Romans presumed that by taking extraordinary security measures, they could prevent a theft (they certainly didn't take the resurrection prophecy by Jesus seriously).

> The next day, the one after Preparation Day, the chief priests and the Pharisees went to Pilate. "Sir," they said, "we remember that while he was still alive that deceiver said, 'After three days I will rise again.' So give the order for the tomb to be made secure until the third day. Otherwise, his disciples may come and steal the body and tell the people that he has been raised from the dead. This last deception will be worse than the first."
>
> "Take a guard," Pilate answered. "Go, make the tomb as secure as you know how" (Matthew 27:62-65).

Posting of a Roman Guard

Thousands of people were turning to Jesus, and it had been increasing ever since Jesus delivered Lazarus from the dead. The Jewish leaders recognized that things could get out of hand if somehow Jesus' body could be smuggled away, perhaps placing the disciples in a position of religious power. Pilate immediately granted the request to post a guard.

When analyzing the issue of the guard posted at Jesus' tomb, some people have wondered if the guard posted was a temple guard, not a Roman guard as is often assumed. But even the temple guard members were highly trained. The temple guard would have consisted of about ten men—any one of whom would have been executed if he fell asleep at an inappropriate time. However, evidence overwhelmingly suggests that a Roman guard was dispatched to guard the body of Jesus, for the following reasons:

1. In the Bible, the Greek word *koustodia* (guard) is used, which at the time referred to a Roman guard.

2. Pilate issued the order, implying he was in ultimate command of the guard. (If only a temple guard were requested, why would the Pharisees have gone to Pilate to request help?).

3. When the guards approached the Jewish religious leaders after the resurrection, they were obviously concerned about the reaction of Pilate—not the religious leaders themselves. This is evident by the Jewish leaders' stating: "If this report [i.e., the report of the guards sleeping] gets to the governor, we will satisfy him and keep you out of trouble" (Matthew 28:14). If it were only a temple guard, which was under the authority of the religious leaders, serious consequences would have been faced immediately. In this case, the religious leaders were sought out to try to avoid a sentence of execution that might be issued by the Roman authorities.

The Roman guard would have consisted of 16 soldiers for an important political prisoner like Jesus. These guards were typically arranged four on each side of whatever they were to protect. At night, four guards would have been placed directly in front of the entrance to the tomb with the other 12 sleeping "face in" in a semicircle in front of the four that were at watch. Guards slept in shifts so that there would always be a minimum of four on watch at a time. Any guard who deserted his post or fell asleep would face crucifixion.[1]

The Two-Ton Stone

The biblical historical record indicates that a stone covered the entrance to the tomb of Jesus, and it was a formidable barrier:

> When the Sabbath was over, Mary Magdalene, Mary the mother of James, and Salome bought spices so that they might go to anoint Jesus' body. Very early on the first day of the week, just after sunrise, they were on their way to the tomb and they asked each other, "Who will roll the stone away from the entrance of the tomb?" (Mark 16:1-3).

Scholars estimate that the stone enclosing the tomb of Jesus weighed about two tons. It was typical of the stones that were used in burial tombs at the time.

Some critics suggest a rather outlandish alternative to the story of the disciples stealing the body. They say that Jesus never died, but simply regained his strength and rolled the stone away. But if he had not died, he most certainly would have been very weak. Additionally, it would have been logistically impossible for him to move the stone from inside the tomb. Not only was the weight far too heavy, but since the stone covered the opening, he wouldn't be able to find a handhold. For others outside the tomb, it could be moved with enough strength. But it was an obstacle to be reckoned with, as shown by the concern of the women approaching the tomb the day of the resurrection.

The Seal Protecting the Tomb

One of the security measures taken was to attach a seal to the stone covering the entrance to the tomb: "So they went and made the tomb secure by putting a seal on the stone and posting the guard" (Matthew 27:66).

The seal was a cord stretched across the entrance to the tomb with a waxlike connection in the middle that would have prevented the opening of the tomb without breaking the bond. The "seal" of the administrative authority in charge was pressed into the wax signifying its importance. Only the captain of the guard was permitted to give permission for the breaking of the seal. Anyone breaking it without permission would be executed.

Certainly the seal alone was breakable and could be easily overcome. However, it did provide a psychological barrier to rolling away the stone without permission. It also reinforced the significant importance of protecting the grave site from opening without agreement by the Romans.

Overall Impact of Security Precautions at the Tomb

No doubt the security precautions at Jesus' tomb were widely known. It would have been impossible for anyone to tamper with the tomb without the knowledge and approval of those charged with protecting it. Overcoming a Roman guard of 16 soldiers, moving a two-ton rock, and breaking a seal that would have meant certain death—all of these measures helped ensure that the body of Jesus would not be disturbed without the Romans knowing about it.

CONCLUSION

The high security at the tomb of Jesus provides assurance that the empty tomb was in fact due to the resurrection of Jesus, not due to a theft or any other form of disturbance.

The Martyrdom of the Apostles

S alome, with uncontrollable sobbing and tears in her eyes clung tightly to her husband, Zebedee. She'd seen it before. She'd seen what someone with absolute power can do. First it was her Lord, Jesus himself. Then it was Stephen, who gave up his spirit as people threw stone after stone (Acts 7:54-60). Now it was her eldest son, James, a disciple of Jesus, who was being dragged through the streets like a piece of garbage to be disposed of. Salome knew she should be forgiving, but this was her own son. She held King Herod Agrippa I in angry contempt.

Finally they reached the site of execution. Then a shocking event happened. To everyone's astonishment, one of the Roman guards suddenly fell to his knees and cried out to James for forgiveness. He had seen such incredible courage from James that he too began to weep uncontrollably and asked James to allow him to be permitted into the kingdom of God.

"Don't kill him alone," the guard said. "Take me too. James, quickly, tell me what to do!"

"Just believe in Jesus and accept him as your Lord and Savior," James cried as his head was carefully being placed on the executioner's block. Seconds rushed by and Zebedee held Salome ever so tightly with feigned strength. She didn't want to look. Oh, how she didn't want to look. But this was her last chance to see her son.

James looked over at his mother with a sense of serenity and deep love that only a mother would recognize. He smiled. And then it was over.

THE EARLY WRITER CLEMENS ALEXANDRINUS documented this story of the execution of James, the elder brother of the apostle John and son of Zebedee and Salome; The story reveals the enormous courage of the early apostles who faced cruel death on a daily basis simply for believing in Jesus and spreading his truth.

But this story of James is not an isolated case of martyrdom by the disciples. All of them, except John, would face a similar fate. All died horrible, cruel deaths simply because they believed in and spread the gospel message.[1]

Peter

After Jesus' crucifixion Peter was despondent. If Jesus really had remained dead and not been resurrected, one would expect Peter to return to the life of a fisherman. After all, he was an expert in fishing, but he was a rather rough, unpolished public speaker. Yet Peter immediately launched into a highly uncharacteristic career as an apostle and never returned to fishing. Obviously the resurrection changed his life forever. And Peter would have certainly been in a position to know whether or not the resurrection was real. He had just spent about three years with Jesus on a daily basis. He was there the night before and the day of the crucifixion. And Peter was among the first to see the resurrected Christ.

Peter started his new career by giving emboldened speeches that persuaded thousands of local Jews to follow the risen Christ. Although Peter started his evangelism in Jerusalem, he soon left to spread the message elsewhere, after having been imprisoned twice. History indicates that he traveled to preach in Corinth for a short time after Paul had established a church there.

The historian Eusebius states that Peter established the Syrian Church in Antioch shortly after the resurrection. Church tradition holds that Peter continued in leadership as its first bishop from A.D. 33 to 40. During that time, he ministered to the region of Mesopotamia, a region of strength and importance for the Jews. It is likely that Peter continued his missionary work in Babylon and the eastern region for many of the remaining years leading up to his death in A.D. 67, although there is considerable evidence that during that time he also spent time in Great Britain, Gaul, and Rome.

Although Peter undoubtedly faced the ongoing persecution common to Christians during his years of ministry, the brutality he endured at the end of his life is an amazing testimony in the strength of his faith in the resurrection of Jesus. Nero had declared himself the "enemy of God" and was bent on promoting this pride-filled position. He, therefore, had every reason to maximize treachery of Christians—especially the leaders like Peter and Paul.

Peter was maliciously condemned and thrown into the infamous Mamertine Prison in Rome. Mamertine was a deep dark vault carved into solid rock, consisting of two chambers, one atop the other. A narrow slit on the roof provided the only access and light to the upper chamber. The lower chamber, known as the "death cell," was in total darkness, and was never cleaned. A horrid stench filled the prison that was so great that it fatally poisoned many inmates.

In the Mamertine "living hell," Peter was chained upright to a post, in a physically exhausting position that didn't allow him to recline to rest. There, alone, wallowing in filth, in total darkness, Peter awaited his death for nine long months—the monotony broken only by periods of intense torture. All Peter had to do to be set free was to renounce Jesus. But the gospel spread as Nero continued to build his personal claim as the enemy of God.

One day in A.D. 67, Peter was led into Nero's circus to be executed. There Peter demanded that he be crucified head down as he was not fit to be crucified in the same position as his Lord Jesus Christ. The taunting Romans granted his request.

As Peter was led away to be crucified, he looked over at his wife, who likewise was being led away to be executed. In his volume *Church History,* Eusebius quotes Peter's last words of encouragement to his wife, "O thou, remember the Lord."

Rather than submit to Roman authorities, who tried using every means to break Peter's spirit and to have him renounce the resurrection, Peter remained firm—as did his wife—and faced horrendous hardships to glorify Jesus. Certainly Peter knew the truth of the resurrection. Would he and his wife have gone through this for a known lie?

Andrew

Andrew was the first person to be approached as a follower of Jesus. He was present at the first miracle and many thereafter. Andrew knew Jesus very well and would certainly have known if, in fact, Jesus actually appeared alive after the crucifixion. Andrew's evangelical actions following the resurrection demonstrate his belief that Jesus was, in fact, the Son of God.

There are several nonbiblical accounts of the ministry of Andrew following the resurrection. While they differ in some respects, there are many points of agreement. It is not certain when Andrew left Jerusalem to spread the gospel. He is believed to have spent most of his ministry in Scythia, in southern Russia, around the Black Sea (from Eusebius). Other sources indicate that Andrew also spent time evangelizing in Asia Minor in the city of Ephesus, where some people believe John's gospel was written, based in part, to a revelation given to Andrew.[2] It is possible the time spent in Asia Minor was following Andrew's ministry to Scythia, while Andrew was on his way to Greece, where sources generally agree that he spent his final years and was executed.

In Patras, Greece, tradition (as confirmed by several nonbiblical sources) indicates that Andrew angered the governor of the region because he converted the governor's wife to Christianity, causing their estrangement. As a consequence, the governor had Andrew crucified on a cross in the form of an "X," not the traditional cross of Jesus. (This form of cross is now referred to as the St. Andrew's cross.)

Like Paul and other apostles, Andrew endured torture prior to his execution. Instead of being nailed to the cross, like others, Andrew was tied in order to prolong the suffering. Hour after hour he bore extreme pain and humiliation while being exposed to the elements with no clothing on. Even so, during this time it is recorded that Andrew exhorted Christians and other onlookers, praising God. His torture went on for two days until he finally succumbed to death on the last day of November in approximately A.D. 69. Andrew's last words were said to have been, "Accept me, oh Christ Jesus, whom I love, whose I am; accept my spirit in peace in your eternal realm."

Thomas

The apostle Thomas is best known for his doubting of the resurrection of Jesus: "Unless I see the nail marks in his hands and put my finger where the nails were, and put my hand into his side, I will not believe it" (John 20:25). However, this doubting turned into determined commitment once he did encounter the risen Christ. After leaving Jerusalem, Thomas traveled east to Babylon and beyond to India where he became known as the founder of the Church of the East. His ministry is said to have started in about A.D. 52 in the city of Crangamore. Ancient records indicate that he didn't want to serve in India due to the harshness of the environment, yet chose to follow his calling by Jesus anyway.

Details of Thomas' ministry vary, but accounts generally agree regarding his martyrdom. Apparently Thomas had discredited the Brahmins, a Hindu sect, before the king. They became envious of his missionary success and set out to kill him. It is reported that one day Thomas was deep in prayer in a cave on the slopes of Mount Antenodur. The Brahmins attacked him, tortured him, thrust a spear through his side, and then fled. Thomas left the cave in agony and dragged himself up the slope where he died.

Matthew

Tradition has it that Matthew traveled to Ethiopia and became associated with Candace (e.g., Acts 8:27). Reports of his martyrdom vary. The Jewish Talmud indicates he was condemned by the Sanhedrin. Some writings indicate he was pinned to the ground and beheaded for his faith in about A.D. 60.

Philip

Philip traveled into Scythia (southern Russia) soon after the resurrection. There he preached the gospel for 20 years. Some reports indicate that he also spent time in Gaul (France); however, they are not confirmed.

Records indicate that Philip was martyred at the age of 87 in the city of Hierapolis in Phrygia. It is reported that pagan priests crucified him upside down by piercing him through the thighs. He was then stoned as he hung upon the cross. In his dying moments, Philip is said to have prayed, like Jesus did, for his enemies before yielding up his spirit.

Bartholomew (Nathaniel)

Bartholomew is always named along with Philip in the Gospels. Following the resurrection, he traveled with Philip to Scythia where they worked together in Hierapolis. Bartholomew escaped crucifixion, however, at the time Philip was crucified.

From Hierapolis, Bartholomew traveled to Armenia, where he is said to have started the Christian Church in that region. He was martyred at Albana (now Derbend, Russia). One account indicates that pagan priests and the king's brother, Astyages, became hostile as Bartholomew spoke out against the local idols (and healed the king's daughter). Bartholomew's enemies eventually were able to have him arrested, beaten, and crucified in A.D. 68.

Jude Thaddaeus

Sometimes the names of the 12 disciples are confusing. For example, Jude appears in some cases and Thaddaeus in others. However, Thaddaeus was the surname of Jude. The ancient historian Jerome refers to him as "Trionius," which means the man with three names. (e.g., Judas Thaddaeus Lebbaeus—Matthew 10:3 NKJV). He was the son of James (Luke 6:16).

The early church historian Nicephorus Callistus reviews the ministry of Jude in Syria, Arabia, Mesopotamia, and Persia. Other sources document extensive involvement of Jude with the Armenian Church from A.D. 35–43. It is believed that he served with Bartholomew and Thomas in the region for several years. Sources indicate that Jude was martyred by a barrage of arrows on Mount Ararat.

James, Son of Alphaeus

James, son of Alphaeus and often called "James the Less," is sometimes confused with James, the brother of Jesus. Much of this confusion stems from early Roman Catholic and Armenian Orthodox attempts to utilize obscure Greek references to demonstrate that both were one and the same person in order to explain the perpetual virginity of Mary (which the church felt was important at the time when all sexual intercourse was considered evil). These explanations, however, fall short in that they must consider James the Less as either: 1) a brother with two sisters named "Mary" in the same family; or 2) a half-brother (not scripturally correct); or 3) a "cousin" (which meant Paul chose the wrong word). None of these seems a satisfactory answer.

Separating James, son of Alphaeus, and James, Jesus' brother, makes it much easier to understand the Scripture and much easier to research. Sources indicate that James the Less traveled to Syria soon after the resurrection where he became the first bishop of the Syrian Church. (Jesus' brother James, on the other hand, became the chairman of the church of Jerusalem.) Tradition further indicates that James the Less later returned to Jerusalem, where he was stoned to death by the Jews for preaching the gospel of Christ.

Simon the Zealot

Simon became a disciple at the Sea of Tiberius, along with Andrew, Peter, James (the Great), John, Thaddaeus, and Judas Iscariot. There are many ancient documents that record the ministry of Simon following the resurrection. Though differing in details, they indicate that Simon first began his missionary work in Egypt and North Africa. From there he traveled to Carthage,

Spain, and North Britain. After a short stay, he traveled to London and went back to Palestine.

Simon then is believed to have traveled to Persia where records indicate he evangelized with Jude. Ancient documents describe Simon as having to endure "infinite troubles and difficulties." In Persia, Simon was eventually sawn in two for preaching about the resurrection of Jesus.

John

Of the 12 disciples, only John died a natural death.

Other Apostles (not of the Twelve) Who Were Martyred

James, brother of Jesus—James was the early leader of the church in Jerusalem (Acts 12:17; 15:13-29; 21:18-24) and the author of the book of James. The Jewish historian Josephus records the martyrdom of James by stoning. It is believed to have occurred in about A.D. 66.

Matthias—Matthias was elected to fill the vacancy created by Judas. It is said he was stoned and then beheaded.

Mark—Tradition indicates that Mark was dragged to pieces in Alexandria after speaking out against the local idol Serapis.

Paul—Paul had spent a great deal of time in the prisons of Rome where he wrote many of his epistles. In A.D. 66 Emperor Nero condemned Paul to death and had him beheaded.

Barnabas—Barnabas spread the gospel to many countries, yet on a return to Cyprus he was martyred by the Jews for his evangelism. History records that John Mark secretly buried his body in an empty sepulcher outside the city of Salamis.

Who Would Die for a Lie?

Fact 1 — All of these apostles (except Paul and Barnabas) knew Jesus intimately *before* he was crucified. (Paul and Barnabas may have seen Jesus before his crucifixion also.) There would be absolutely no doubt about their ability to recognize Jesus and distinguish between him and any other person who might simply look like him.

Fact 2 — All of the twelve (and others) saw Jesus *after* his resurrection from the dead.

Fact 3 — All of the apostles *changed radically* after seeing the risen Christ—from being rather withdrawn followers to being bold speakers and leaders.

Fact 4 — All apostles *started preaching* the good news about the death and resurrection of Jesus—an action that threatened their lives.

Fact 5 — All apostles *would have had their lives spared* by simply renouncing Jesus and stopping their evangelism.

Fact 6 — All of the apostles willingly, even joyfully, *laid down their lives* in most horrible, painful ways, to spread the good news about Jesus' death and resurrection.

Why Did They Willingly Die?

The obvious question by an outside, objective observer would be, "Why would people willingly endure horrible executions when they could avoid it by a simple renunciation of their faith?" The only answer is that they were *absolutely, totally convinced that Jesus died and rose from the dead,* verifying his claim to be the Son of God.

When people question the authenticity of the account of the resurrection, they should consider that in the case of the apostles, we have at least ten people, *who certainly knew the truth* and decided to choose death over rejecting Jesus. If Jesus' resurrection was a lie, why would they die? Some people say these followers of Jesus were insane. But is it likely that *all ten* were insane? Or was Jesus just an illusion? Would all the disciples see the same illusion at once? Hardly.

Furthermore, the apostles were martyred over a long period of time and in various locations. There wasn't a mass execution. This indicates the continuing conviction they held. It wasn't a short-term belief of little consequence; it was considered a life-changing belief that was of enormous importance.

CONCLUSION

The martyrdom of the apostles, who knew Jesus intimately, is a powerful example of eyewitnesses who were absolutely convinced that Jesus Christ died and rose again from the dead, just as he prophesied he would. Any of the martyred apostles could have easily chosen to avoid execution by renouncing Jesus. None of them did. The disciples died so that others might believe in Christ and live.

The Witnesses of Spectacular Events of Jesus

Did you hear what happened?" shrieked Doris, her voice breaking through sob after sob as tears streamed down her face. Her friend Anne ran to comfort the obviously shaken 24-year-old.

"What on earth's the matter?" Anne asked.

"It's the World Trade Center! It's totally destroyed! Absolutely destroyed...All of it...Both buildings!" screamed Doris.

"Impossible!" Anne interjected. "Surely you're mistaken. Just calm down."

"No, it's true!" Doris yelled. "Planes were hijacked, then flown into the buildings like kamikaze missiles that exploded into the towers!

"It was horrible. I saw people jumping to their deaths a hundred stories high as flames streaked skyward! Then the buildings collapsed into mountains of rubble."

The story went on and on and was told in detail after graphic detail. Doris was beside herself. She told Anne. Anne told Bob. Bob told Sherri. And so on, and so on, and so on. Such a memorable event, with such vivid detail—it would never be forgotten by any of the witnesses. And the conviction of the witnesses would be believed by others. People glued their eyes to television, newspapers, and anything else to gather information about the heart-wrenching events of September 11, 2001.

WE CAN UNDERSTAND TODAY HOW MEMORABLE an event such as the World Trade Center attack would be. Why would anyone suppose for even a second that the events surrounding Jesus Christ were any less significant to the people at the time? The only difference would be that they would not have mass media to communicate what the eyewitnesses saw. In Jesus' time, the people would talk to eyewitnesses themselves or to others who were credible sources of eyewitness testimony. The resurrection of Jesus might well have been regarded as shocking then as the World Trade Center attack is today.

The importance of the memorability of incredible events is that it burns vivid detail into the minds of those witnessing them. Consequently, the facts are not forgotten, and discussed stories can easily be compared. Eventually when they are recorded, as in the New Testament, the accuracy of the writings are easily verified.

While the resurrection of Jesus was certainly the highlight, there were also many other extraordinary things that happened concerning Jesus.

Miraculous Birth of John the Baptist

Zechariah saw an angel who foretold that his wife, Elizabeth, would conceive and bear a son. When Zechariah questioned the heavenly messenger, the angel said the man would lose his speech until it came to pass.

> Meanwhile, *the people* were waiting for Zechariah and wondering why he stayed so long in the temple. When he came out, he could not speak to them. They realized he had seen a vision in the temple, for he kept making signs to them but remained unable to speak (Luke 1:21-22).

Zechariah was old and his wife, Elizabeth, was past the child-bearing years. Yet they were promised the birth of John (the Baptist)—a promise that was miraculously fulfilled.

> Your wife Elizabeth will bear you a son, and you are to give him the name John....Zechariah asked the angel, "How can I be sure of this? I am an old man and my wife is well along in years" (Luke 1:13-14,18).

After Elizabeth's child was born and when he was to be named eight days later, Elizabeth said his name would be John. Zechariah confirmed this and his speech was restored.

Supernatural Announcement of Jesus' Birth

Angels supernaturally announced the birth of Jesus.

> An angel of the Lord appeared to them, and the glory of the Lord shone around them, and *they* [the shepherds] were terrified. But the angel said to them, "Do not be afraid. I bring you good news of great joy that will be for all the people. Today in the town of David a Savior has been born to you; he is Christ the Lord. This will be a sign to you: You will find a baby wrapped in cloths and lying in a manger." Suddenly a great company of the heavenly host appeared with the angel, praising God... (Luke 2:9-13).

… When they had seen him, *they spread the word* concerning what had been told them about this child, and *all who heard it* were amazed at what the shepherds said to them (Luke 2:17-18).

Recognition of Jesus as Messiah by Respected Elder

People marveled at the public recognition of Jesus as the Messiah by Simeon.

Moved by the Spirit, [Simeon] went into the *temple courts.* When the parents brought in the child Jesus to do for him what the custom of the Law required, Simeon took him in his arms and praised God, saying: "Sovereign Lord, as you have promised, you now dismiss your servant in peace. For my eyes have seen your salvation, which you have prepared in the sight of all people, a light for revelation to the Gentiles and for glory to your people Israel." The child's father and mother marveled at what was said about him (Luke 2:27-33).

Recognition of Jesus as Messiah by Respected Prophetess

People were also moved by the public recognition of Jesus as the Messiah by Anna, a respected prophetess.

There was also a prophetess, Anna, the daughter of Phanuel, of the tribe of Asher. She was very old; she had lived with her husband seven years after her marriage, and then was a widow until she was eighty-four. *She never left the temple* but worshiped night and day, fasting and praying. Coming up to them at that very moment, she gave thanks to God and spoke about the child *to all who were looking forward to the redemption of Jerusalem* (Luke 2:36-38).

Supernatural Warning to Flee to Egypt

Joseph and Mary were warned supernaturally by an angel to flee to Eygpt.

> When they had gone, an angel of the Lord appeared to Joseph in a dream. "Get up," he said, "take the child and his mother and escape to Egypt. Stay there until I tell you, for Herod is going to search for the child to kill him." So he got up, took the child and his mother during the night and left for Egypt, where he stayed until the death of Herod (Matthew 2:13-15).

Herod's Killing of Babies

Although not a spectacular, noteworthy event from a historical viewpoint, the murder of 15 to 30 babies by Herod certainly would have impacted the local population. So Herod ordering the killing of all male babies under two years old in the Bethlehem area was significant.

> When Herod realized that he had been outwitted by the Magi, he was furious, and he gave orders to kill *all the boys in Bethlehem and its vicinity* who were two years old and under, in accordance with the time he had learned from the Magi (Matthew 2:16).

The Many Miracles of Jesus

There were many miracles of Jesus mentioned in the Bible, any of which would be highly memorable.

The Crucifixion of Jesus

The crucifixion of Jesus would be highly memorable because it was tied to an individual with a known reputation for miracles and because the person had indicated that he would rise again from the dead.

The Resurrection of Jesus

The resurrection of Jesus has been proven to be, arguably, the most memorable event of all time.

The Miracles Performed by the Disciples

The many miracles performed by the apostles would be highly memorable (Acts 2:43; 5:12). For example:

> Now a man crippled from birth was being carried to the temple gate called Beautiful, where he was put every day to beg from those going into the *temple courts*....Then Peter said, "Silver or gold I do not have, but what I have I give you. In the name of Jesus Christ of Nazareth, walk." Taking him by the right hand, he helped him up, and instantly the man's feet and ankles became strong. He jumped to his feet and began to walk. Then he went with them into the *temple courts,* walking and jumping, and praising God. When *all the people saw him* walking and praising God, they recognized him as the same man who used to sit begging at the temple gate called Beautiful, and *they were filled with wonder and amazement* at what had happened to him (Acts 3:2,6-10).

The Resurrected Appearance of Jesus to 500

After the resurrection Jesus appeared before 500 people.

> For what I received I passed on to you as of first importance: that Christ died for our sins according to the Scriptures, that he was buried, that he was raised on

the third day according to the Scriptures, and that he appeared to Peter, and then to the Twelve. After that, he appeared to more than five hundred of the brothers at the same time, most of whom are still living, though some have fallen asleep (1 Corinthians 15:3-6).

People Talked

People in Jesus' day were not unlike today. They loved to talk. In fact, one would expect that with fewer distractions such as TV, computers, and video games, they probably talked even more than today.

Every one of the events just mentioned was far from ordinary. Each one was highly memorable. These events were *witnessed* by many people and were widely *discussed* throughout the land. Like the events of September 11, 2001, they would be remembered vividly by many people for a long period of time. The people would also have been able to easily corroborate written reports in the New Testament, thus verifying the accuracy. People widely discussing memorable events of the day would validate the essentials of the events. The truth would withstand eyewitness scrutiny; the rest would be discarded.

Information Sources for the Gospels

Luke used information from many sources to research the gospel message.

> Many have undertaken to draw up an account of the things that have been fulfilled among us, just as they were handed down to us by those who from the first were eyewitnesses and servants of the word. Therefore, since I myself have *carefully investigated everything* from the beginning, it seemed good also to me to write

an orderly account for you, most excellent Theophilus,
so that you may *know the certainty* of the things you
have been taught (Luke 1:1-4).

Notice that the historian Luke, called one of the greatest historians of all time by one of the greatest archaeologists of all time—Sir William Ramsay, indicated that he did a *methodical* investigation of the account of the story of Jesus.

Mary

The Virgin Mary, mother of Jesus, is without a doubt the most revered mother of all time. When one considers the evidence surrounding the birth, life, death, and resurrection of Jesus, nobody would be in a position to know the full story better than Mary. She was there for almost everything—except for the rigorous journeys during the three-year ministry of Jesus (and even then, there was probably some contact).

People would have talked about the many miraculous events surrounding Jesus' birth, life, and death. Mary was there at the annunciation of the coming of Jesus by angels. She was there at the conception of Jesus. She was there at the miraculous birth, announced by angels appearing to shepherds. She was there when an angel warned Joseph to flee to Egypt. She was nearby when Herod mercilessly slaughtered the infant boys in the region of Bethlehem. She was there when Jesus performed the many miracles, and she is specifically mentioned when Jesus performed his first miracle of turning water into wine (John 2:1-11). She was there at Jesus' crucifixion, standing beneath him at the cross:

> Near the cross of Jesus stood his mother, his
> mother's sister, Mary the wife of Clopas, and Mary
> Magdalene. When Jesus saw his mother there, and the
> disciple whom he loved standing nearby, he said to his
> mother, "Dear woman, here is your son," and to the

disciple, "Here is your mother." From that time on, this disciple took her into his home (John 19:25-27).

And she was there at the time of the resurrection of Jesus (Acts 1:14). The evidence of Mary's involvement is apparent with the many churches that were immediately built at the venerated sites where she was a participant soon after Constantine allowed Christianity in the Roman Empire. This indicates that the local population was well aware of the events and of Mary's role. The belief in Mary and her involvement has not diminished with time.

The gospel authors almost certainly used Mary as one of their original sources of information.

Conon—A Direct Relative of Jesus

Gospel authors would have certainly gathered information from the relatives of Jesus. We know that such relatives existed. It was difficult to maintain the lineage of Jesus given the persecution that occurred shortly after the resurrection because one would expect that most of the ancestors of Jesus would be martyred. The last recorded ancestor of Jesus was a gardener named Conon who lived in Pamphylia in Asia Minor. Just prior to his death, Conon was asked if he was of the lineage of King David. He replied, "I am of the city of Nazareth in Galilee, I am of the family of Christ, whose worship I have inherited from my ancestors."[1]

Other Relatives of Jesus

The Bible indicates that Jesus had brothers and sisters: "Isn't his mother's name Mary, and aren't his brothers James, Joseph, Simon and Judas? Aren't all his sisters with us?" (Matthew 13:55).

Roman Catholicism teaches that these relatives are actually cousins or brothers and sisters from a previous marriage of

Joseph. Protestants and most biblical scholars, however, believe they were natural siblings of Jesus. Either way, Jesus had brothers and sisters or relatives who would be used by gospel authors to corroborate facts about Jesus' life, death, and resurrection.

Apart from mention of relatives in the Bible, we find mention of other relatives in extrabiblical sources. The great historian Eusebius, who wrote at the time of Constantine (c. A.D. 300) mentions two grandsons of Jude, the brother of Jesus, who were brought before Emperor Domitian in the fifteenth year of his reign (the year 95). They were freed when they admitted to being from the house of David. They then started several churches in the area "because they were relatives of the Lord."

Eusebius also writes of Symeon, son of Clopas (who was thought to be Joseph's brother—see John 19:25), who succeeded James as church leader and was martyred at the age of 120.[2] Hegesippus, who wrote in about A.D. 170, described the lengthy torture and eventual martyrdom of Symeon—in a manner similar to that of Jesus. He writes:

> Certain of these heretics brought accusation against Symeon, the son of Clopas, on the ground that he was a descendant of David and a Christian; and thus he suffered martyrdom, at the age of one hundred and twenty years, while Trajan was emperor and Atticus governor."[3]

Hegesippus also briefly refers to the same grandsons of Jude mentioned by Eusebius.

James, Brother of Jesus

The Bible refers to James (and Jude) as brothers of Jesus:

> "I saw none of the other apostles—only James, the Lord's brother (Galatians 1:19).

Jude, a servant of Jesus Christ and a brother of James (Jude 1).

However we also find evidence of Jesus' brother James outside the Bible, including what may be his actual ossuary (see pages 144-146). But evidence of the existence and role of James, brother of Jesus, goes beyond the ossuary. Josephus (a non-Christian, Jewish historian, c. 37-96) speaks of the execution of James:

> Albinus...assembled the Sanhedrim of the judges, and brought before them the brother of Jesus, who was called Christ, whose name was James, and some others [or some of his companions;] and when he had formed an accusation against them as breakers of the law, he delivered them to be stoned...."[4]

The noncanonical "Gospel of Thomas" (see pages 112-113) written c. A.D. 140[5] speaks of James as "the Lord's brother, who had been elected by the Apostles to the Episcopal throne at Jerusalem."[6] Other writings that speak of James and his election to lead the church of Jerusalem include: the Syriac Apostolic Constitutions (second century), Clement of Rome (A.D. 30–97), Hegesippus (A.D. 100–180), Eusebius of Caesarea (A.D. 260–340), Clement of Alexandria (A.D. 150–215, surviving in a document by Eusebius), Origen (A.D. 185–254), and Jerome (A.D. 342–420).

Mary Magdelene, the "Other Mary," and Salome

Mary, the "other Mary," and Salome were three women who were closely involved in the life of Jesus (see Mark 15:40; 16:1). We know that by the fact that they were going to the tomb to finish preparing Jesus' body the day of the resurrection; hence, they were intimately involved in the many events on that fateful day. Most certainly the gospel writers would have obtained eyewitness testimony from these three loyal women, along with any others like them.

500 Persons Seeing the Resurrected Jesus

We know that in at least one instance Jesus appeared to 500 people at once (1 Corinthians 15:3-7). What is particularly significant is that Paul is reporting this fact to the Corinthians in a letter sometime prior to A.D. 64, when it is stated that many of them (the eyewitnesses) are still alive. Since this letter to the Corinthians was copied and passed around to a wide audience throughout the Roman Empire, it most certainly was "reviewable" by some of the eyewitnesses themselves. This means that if it were incorrect, it would have been challenged. Yet it was not—and it remains in the most widely read book of all time, the Bible.

THROUGHOUT THE PERIOD OF JESUS' BIRTH, ministry, death, and resurrection, there were many incredible reasons for people to remember spectacular events and discuss them. As we've seen, Matthew, Mark, Luke, and John would have no trouble finding eyewitnesses to corroborate the Gospels. And if there had been any inconsistencies in the widely discussed accounts, there would have been criticism and correction since written copies were circulated during the time of the eyewitnesses (see chapter 9).

CONCLUSION

There were many highly memorable events during Jesus' time, capped by his resurrection. These would certainly gain attention and would be widely discussed. The many witnesses of the events and the resurrection—including the apostles, the friends and family of Jesus, and at least 500 others who saw the risen Christ—would attest to his resurrection.

Hostile Witnesses

The wind moaned through the trees in an eerie song that forebode the bloodshed to come. A damp mist clung to his face as the battle-worn emperor slumped to his knees deep in thought outside an army camp a few miles north of Rome. It was October 28, 312. Carved in his mind were words he had heard from his Christian mother, Helena, since childhood: "Give to Caesar what is Caesar's, and to God what is God's" (Matthew 22:21).

Slowly Emperor Constantine raised his head and saw through the mist an apparition. Seemingly coming from an infinite distance he saw a vision of a cross of light above the sun bearing an inscription—"Conquer by this." Word quickly spread throughout the camp as the many soldiers excitedly related their versions of sighting the same apparition.

Later in the day, after a fitful sleep, Constantine had a second vision. The "Christ of God" appeared to him with the same sign and commanded him to make a likeness of it to use as a safeguard in all battles. It was to have a spear with a transverse bar giving it the shape of a cross; the Greek letters X and P intersecting within a golden wreath on the point of the spear forming the monogram Chi-Rho, the first two letters of Christ in Greek.

Stunned by the vision, the Emperor Constantine sent for Christian leaders. Surely they expected to be executed by the pagan emperor. However, far from executing them, Constantine asked their advice regarding the "God of the Christians." In his discussions he received information about the incarnation and immortality of Christ.

Constantine obeyed the command. Battle standards were made. Uplifting them with the sudden cry that Constantine could not be defeated, the army brandished their swords as their enemy Maxentius and his soldiers crossed a bridge of boats to meet them. Earlier in the day, Maxentius had consulted an oracle that indicated the Roman army of Constantine would be soundly defeated. It was destined to be a battle of the newly received Christian God against the pagan god of Maxentius.

The intensity of the inspired Romans was overwhelming. Constantine's army charged Maxentius' troops, destroyed the bridge behind them, and forced them into the Tiber where they "went to the depths like a stone." The world was changed forever.

HOSTILE WITNESSES HAVE LONG BEEN REGARDED in courts of law to be among the most compelling because when they make significant points supporting the claim of a side they are opposed to (or were opposed to), they are very credible. In this chapter, we review hostile witnesses from three most unique and unusual viewpoints: 1) from the viewpoint of a Roman emperor, originally bent on defeating Christianity, 2) from the viewpoint of a Pharisee originally impassioned to annihilate Christians, and 3) from the blood relatives of Jesus, who at first did not believe in Jesus' divinity.

Emperor Constantine

Few events have changed world history to a greater extent than Constantine's visions, as just described. The historian Eusebius claimed that Constantine recounted his experience and "confirmed it with an oath." There is no doubt that Eusebius had lengthy conversations with Constantine—they are well documented historically.

At the time Constantine was embattled with Maxentius, tax breaks were being offered to cities that uncovered Christians for execution. The fraudulent, infamous "Memoranda of Pilate" was being circulated throughout the Roman Empire to whip up hatred toward Christians, and prostitutes were being rounded up and forced to create false "confessions" of vile Christian perversions. Christian hatred was everywhere, and persecution was at its peak.

Overnight, Constantine changed all of that. In 313, Constantine, based on his newfound belief in Jesus, entered into a pact with the eastern emperor Licinius. An edict was issued to Christians and all men that anyone could "follow the form of worship each desired." In a sense this allowed the two emperors to "hedge their bets" on the Almighty, supposing that eventually the true God would prevail. And eventually one did.

Emperor Licinius eventually abandoned his pact of joint tolerance and resumed horrific persecution of Christians. Eusebius wrote about the impact it had on the enraged Constantine, who marched out "kindling a great beacon of light" and went to war against Licinius. Licinius was soundly defeated and was strangled to death.

The changes Constantine implemented radically changed the world. In 324, Constantine's influence was expanded from being emperor of Rome to emperor of the entire Roman Empire. Efforts were made immediately to correct the improprieties of the past. Christians illegally held for their faith were released. All property and goods that had been seized from Christians was to be restored immediately—this included property that was held in the name of the church, and for the first time such property was to be "officially recognized." Clergymen were given freedom from civic duties and also some tax breaks. The first day of the week (Sunday) was to be a day of rest. And key holidays were established (such as December 25—Christmas—and probably also Easter and Lent).

Constantine's mother, Helena, who was a devout Christian already, was dispatched to the holy lands to locate key sites to be venerated. This action established many of the important archaeological sites we revere today. Despite all the efforts of Constantine, old feelings about Christians—caused by extensive misinformation by enemies—were slow to die. It wasn't until 391 that Christianity enjoyed a definitive monopoly as a state religion.

During his lifetime, Constantine was wary of alienating his subjects and was cautious about obliterating pagan sites and temples. However, upon his death in A.D. 337, the pace of destroying such sites quickened. Rome, of course, had become the seat of the church that was destined to become the largest religion in the world.

Paul

"Saul of Tarsus" (Paul), was the leading persecutor of Christians in the years immediately following Jesus' crucifixion (Acts 7:57–8:3). He was the overseer at the stoning of Stephen, the first recorded Christian martyr. Saul was his Hebrew name, although in most of the New Testament he is referred to by his Greek name Paul.

Paul took his attack against Christians to Damascus, and he had received "letters of commendation" from the priests in Jerusalem to make his job easier. His goal was to round up Christians and deliver them back to Jerusalem for trial and execution. On the way, he suddenly encountered a blinding light and heard the words of Jesus:

"Saul, Saul, why do you persecute me?"

"Who are you, Lord?" Saul asked.

"I am Jesus, whom you are persecuting," he replied. "Now get up and go into the city, and you will be told what you must do" (Acts 9:4-6).

Paul had been blinded, a condition that was to last for three days—until a man named Ananias, called by God, would go to Paul and restore his sight. Ananias took on this task with great fear, at first, because the reputation of Paul had preceded him and all the followers of Christ in Damascus knew of Paul's deadly mission.

However, Paul's experience upon encountering the risen Christ had made him a changed man. Immediately his mission changed from being one of rounding up Christians for execution to preaching the gospel of Jesus. He then went out to local synagogues and preached that Jesus is the Son of God, to the startled amazement of the Christians in attendance (Acts 9:21). "Yet Saul [Paul] became more and more powerful and baffled the Jews living in Damascus by proving that Jesus is the Christ" (Acts 9:22).

After many days of testifying about Jesus, angry Jews plotted to kill Paul to end this embarrassing change in attitude about Jesus. With the help of local Christians, Paul escaped. His new mission in life was now established; he would become, perhaps, the most influential advocate of Jesus Christ of all time.

For the remainder of Paul's life, he traveled throughout much of the Roman Empire preaching the good news about the resurrection of Jesus. Paul was especially suited for this task. He was a Pharisee and the son of a Pharisee (Acts 23:6). His family was obviously of some wealth, which enabled him to gain Roman citizenship, a status that was highly prized at the time. He had been educated under the tutelage of Gamaliel, who was regarded as one of the leading educators. So Paul came from a position of great status, wealth, and education.

Paul's journeys took him to most of Asia Minor and eventually to Rome. He established great churches in all of his travels. During this time he wrote many letters encouraging churches and instructing them in the teachings of Jesus. These letters became, for the most part, books of the New Testament. *Paul is responsible for writing more books of the New Testament than any other author.*

But Paul's conversion came at a great personal, "earthly" cost. He was beaten many times, shipwrecked, stoned, and left for dead. He traded his great reputation among the established nation of Jews for a leadership role in a ragged band of new believers in Christ. In the end he gave the ultimate sacrifice for Jesus—his life.

Paul's conversion speaks volumes about the historical validity of Jesus and his resurrection. After all, Paul had seen Jesus *after* the resurrection, and as a practicing Pharisee, may very likely have been in Jerusalem at Passover at the time of Jesus' crucifixion. Paul initially was a "hostile witness" influenced, undoubtedly, by the peer pressure of the religious leaders. This is obvious by his rigorous goal to exterminate the fledgling church of Christ. So when the conversion of Paul took place, with a claim to have encountered the risen Christ, it became a powerful message to all who listened. So great was the embarrassment to the Jewish establishment, that they did their best to rid the region of Paul's teaching. But in the end, God prevailed through Paul. Consider those onlookers who witnessed Paul's stern eyes at the stoning of Stephen (Acts 7:57-60). Who would have thought that Paul's words now impact more people for Christ than perhaps any other writer in history!

James and Jude

So much attention is given to Jesus' adult life and his ministry that it's easy to forget that he, along with his brothers and sisters, had a childhood too. One can only wonder what the relationships of this family were really like. After all, Mary, Joseph, and other relatives were well aware Jesus was supposed to be the Savior of the world.

We do know that when Jesus began his ministry, he was rejected in his hometown:

> Coming to his hometown, he began teaching the people in their synagogue, and they were amazed. "Where did this man get this wisdom and these miraculous powers?" they asked. "Isn't this the carpenter's son? Isn't his mother's name Mary, and aren't his brothers James, Joseph, Simon and Judas? Aren't all his sisters with us? Where then did this man get all these things?" And they took offense at him. But Jesus said to them, "Only in his hometown and in his own house is a prophet without honor." And he did not do many miracles there because of their lack of faith (Matthew 13:54-58).

To fully comprehend the reaction to Jesus in Nazareth—including that of two of his brothers, James and Jude—we must look at Jesus' bold claim to deity in the synagogue:

> The scroll of the prophet Isaiah was handed to him. Unrolling it, he found the place where it is written: "The Spirit of the Lord is on me, because he has anointed me to preach good news to the poor. He has sent me to proclaim freedom for the prisoners and recovery of sight for the blind, to release the oppressed, to proclaim the year of the Lord's favor." Then he rolled up the scroll, gave it back to the attendant and sat down. The eyes of everyone in the synagogue were fastened on him,

and he began by saying to them, "Today this scripture is fulfilled in your hearing" (Luke 4:17-21).

This was a clear claim by Jesus that he was the long-awaited Messiah. The reaction by the religious people and the others in Nazareth emphasizes their outrage:

> All the people in the synagogue were furious when they heard this. They got up, drove him out of the town, and took him to the brow of the hill on which the town was built, in order to throw him down the cliff. But he walked right through the crowd and went on his way (Luke 4:28-30).

What makes the eventual reaction of James and Jude so important in regard to evidence of the claim to deity by Jesus, is that:

1. The two knew Jesus since childhood.

2. The two were part of the crowd in Nazareth who rejected him.

3. The two later changed and recognized Jesus as the Messiah.

We know this because both James and Jude wrote books of the New Testament. Also, James was the leader of the early church in Jerusalem. Paul emphasizes the importance of James by referring to the appearance of the resurrected Jesus to him: "Then he appeared to James, then to all the apostles, and last of all he appeared to me also, as to one abnormally born" (1 Corinthians 15:7-8).

The Roman Catholic Church, which has a doctrine of perpetual virginity for Mary, proclaims that James and Jude were not natural siblings of Jesus, but instead either cousins or brothers by a previous marriage of Joseph. The Protestant church and most scholars believe the two were natural brothers of Jesus. Either way, the point is the same. Brothers close to Jesus rejected him early on, then changed their minds after the resurrection.

CONCLUSION

A wide range of hostile witnesses changed their minds after seeing the risen Christ. First, the brothers of Jesus finally accepted him as Lord after the resurrection. Second, Paul who probably had accepted the "official story" of the corpse of Jesus being stolen, had a radical change of mind upon seeing the risen Christ. And finally, after three centuries of Roman persecution of Christians, Emperor Constantine saw a vision of Christ, causing him to end the persecution. Together these hostile witnesses make an exceptionally strong claim that the risen Christ is real.

The Early
Christian Martyrs

The rain fell softly as if tears of Almighty God himself mourned in respect for the martyrs who gave their lives that day defending the name of Christ Jesus. The procession of mourners ambled slowly through the streets outside the gates of Rome until it reached the entrance to the great caves. They hesitated for a moment and sang a hymn of praise to the Father, thanking him for the gift of salvation through Jesus. Andrew reached over to grasp the rain-soaked hand of Rebecca, who had tears streaming down her face. She had just lost her son Cleos at the hands of the Romans. It was 69 years after the crucifixion of Jesus, and Cleos was one of many Christian martyrs who had just been killed.

The horror of the day haunted Andrew. Images burned in his mind—and would be imbedded in his brain for all eternity. Some 47 brothers in the Lord had been rounded up by Roman soldiers to face the wrath of Emperor Trajan. The Christians were referred to as a strange and superstitious cult that sought to undermine the "divine" authority of the emperor by spreading the "superstition" that the "executed criminal, Jesus," was God. One by one, each person was lined up to face Trajan, their accuser. The guards, dressed in armor, solemnly asked each person to do two simple things to be set free: 1) to renounce the name of Jesus and proclaim Trajan as God; 2) to bow down and worship Trajan.

It seemed simple enough.

First went Timothy. A guard firmly grabbed his arm and hurried him forward as Timothy nearly stumbled over his own feet. His eyes glared at the Roman emperor who returned the stare with a rocklike hardness that comes from someone who had sent countless numbers of people to their deaths. When asked to renounce Jesus, there was no hesitation whatsoever, just a confident, firm reply that everyone in attendance could hear "Jesus is Lord." It brought courage to the line of disciples behind him. Then Timothy's hands were tightly bound, and he was led away.

Michael was next. He looked over at his wife and ten-year-old daughter, Anna, as tears streamed down his face. Then he bowed his head in reverence, and sternly proclaimed "Jesus is my God!" One by one, all 47 were queried, and all but Othaniel stood strong in the faith.

The 46 were led to the nearby coliseum where hundreds of people gathered in drunken revelry awaiting the spectacle that was about to occur. Roman guards roughly shoved the tattered group into the center of the great field as the sound of drums echoed a forbidding warning announcing the impending stench of death. In the center of the arena, the group gathered, knelt down, and started singing songs of great joy, praising God and thanking Jesus for the wonderful gift of his sacrifice on the cross. Then the gates opened. Hungry lions sprang forth and charged the group. Lions ripped into the flesh of the 46 frail men. Blood poured from dismembered bodies, staining the ground with its ugly red hue. Songs of joy had turned to uncontrollable screams of terror.

Andrew's thoughts returned to the funeral procession that was making its way to the underground cemetery where the body of Cleos would be laid to rest with the other martyrs awaiting the day that was promised—the day when Jesus would return and the dead would arise.

MUCH LIKE THE DISCIPLES, MANY EARLY CHRISTIANS were in a unique position to know for certain whether or not the story of Jesus was true. Many were eyewitnesses; others knew eyewitnesses. Some witnessed the convicting martyrdom of the disciples and the apostles. Many, many Christians were willing to joyfully give their lives for Christ. As Luke said, they considered it an honor to be considered worthy of suffering for Jesus: "The apostles left the Sanhedrin, rejoicing because they had been counted worthy of suffering disgrace for the Name" (Acts 5:41-42).

The Roman Emperor Nero was the first to encourage Christian persecution on a mass scale. Nero, who had been blamed for the great fire of Rome, attempted to shift the blame to the Christians whom he condemned. Many unimaginable and cruel executions of Christians were devised. Some Christians were sewn inside skins of wild animals and torn at by fierce dogs. Some Christians were dressed in a wax-type shirt, then impaled on poles and set afire to provide light for orgies held on Nero's behalf.

As tales of horror spread throughout the Roman Empire, Nero's strategy to break the spirit of the Christians backfired. Rather than melt away in fear, the spirit of early Christians was strengthened—a sign of their enormous conviction and belief in Christ. Many of the 72 men appointed by Jesus (Luke 10:1) were martyred, including such people as Erastus (Romans 16:23),

Aristarchus (Acts 19:29), Trophimus (Acts 21:29), Barsabbas (Acts 1:23), and Ananias (Acts 9:10).

Ignatius is one later martyr recorded by early church historians. He was a courageous church leader who ministered to many Christians in hiding during the persecution. However, like many Christians at the time, he welcomed the chance to joyously give his life for Christ. When Ignatius realized that he would soon be executed for spreading the gospel of Christ, he said, "[As for the lions ...] I will entice them to devour me quickly....Let come on me fire and cross and conflicts with wild beasts, wrenching of bones, mangling of limbs... only let me reach Jesus Christ."[1]

Later the inevitable happened, and Ignatius was captured and rushed to the coliseum to be executed. He stood spellbound before a bloodthirsty crowd hungry for his demise. Then he looked to the heavens and said, "I am the wheat of Christ: I am going to be ground with the teeth of wild beasts that I may be found pure bread."[2]

The gates were opened and the lions bounded toward him, seemingly in slow motion. Ignatius looked up and joyfully sang songs of praise until the claws finally reached him, the end came, and he was silent. It was A.D. 107.

Nero was the first of a long string of emperors of persecution. Emperor Domitian was the first to issue the order that Christians be brought before the tribunal to be questioned about their faith. All Christians had to do to escape horrific execution was to renounce their faith. Again, they stood strong, willingly facing death instead of renouncing Christ. Among those martyred during this time was Paul's dear friend Timothy (1 Corinthians 4:17).

Emperor Trajan continued the practice of forcing Christians to renounce their faith; however, he added the twist that they also had to bow down to a statue of Trajan and worship him to be set free. Christians continued to choose death.

Trajan was succeeded by Hadrian who was responsible for the deaths of some 10,000 martyrs. He was especially known for placing crowns of thorns on Christians heads, crucifying them, and thrusting spears in their sides in a cruel, mock display of Jesus' crucifixion. This practice, however, *corroborated the written account of Christ's final days.* In one case a Roman commander was asked by Hadrian to join in idolatrous sacrifice to celebrate his victories. When the commander refused due to his faith in Christ, Hadrian had him and his family put to death.

The list of atrocities goes on and on. Perhaps most important to us today is the vast number of martyrs who died during the early years after Jesus. Some would have been in a position to ascertain the truth. *The crux of Christian martyrdom is that it was for a historical event, not merely some philosophical idea like martyrs in other religions.*

Even knowing the truth, how many of us today would willingly face a horrible execution when a "simple renunciation" would forestall it? Certainly the early martyrs had incredible conviction. Fortunately for us, the early martyrs provide compelling evidence that those closest to resurrection—and most likely to know the truth—died because it was of utmost importance to them.

The Catacombs

Anyone visiting Rome today can visit the catacombs, where early Christians buried their dead outside the city of Rome. The catacomb caves are an awe-inspiring testimony to the many early Christian martyrs who gave their lives to spread the gospel of Jesus. Tens of thousands of early Christians were buried in more than 60 underground labyrinths where individual tombs and family crypts were hewn out of narrow rock passageways. (Five of the catacombs are currently open to the public.) Hundreds of miles of tunnels are connected over vast acres of ground, like the strands of a spider's web. In some cases there are many levels of passages to save space, which was very limited for Christians during the time of persecution.

Contrary to popular belief, the catacombs were not used as secret hiding places during persecution; however, at times they were used as places of refuge for celebration of the Lord's Supper.

Standing in one of the open "worship areas" or even in a large "family crypt," one can't help but sense the spirit and powerful commitment to Jesus at a time so close to his crucifixion, when people would have strong evidence of his resurrection. Evidence of early belief in Jesus is everywhere. Symbols are prevalent throughout the catacombs:

1. *The Good Shepherd*—A shepherd with a lamb around his neck, which symbolized Christ and the souls he was saving. This symbol was found in frescoes, on sarcophagi, and on facings of tombs.

2. *The Orante*—A praying figure with open arms symbolizing the soul of the deceased living eternally in peace.

3. *The monogram of Christ*—The Greek letters "X" and "P" which represented the first two letters of "Christ," indicating a Christian was buried there.

4. *The fish*—The Greek letters "IXTHYS," which placed vertically formed an acrostic that stood for "Jesus Christ Son of God Savior."

5. *The dove holding an olive branch*—Symbolizing the soul reaching divine peace.

6. *The Greek letters alpha and omega*—Representing Christ as the beginning and the end.

The thousands of martyrs in the catacombs are often identified by the Greek abbreviation "MPT" (which stood for "martyr").

In February of A.D. 313, Constantine ended the persecution of Christians. However, the catacombs continued to be used as a cemetery until the following century. Eventually the church returned to the practice of above-ground burial. With the passage of time, people forgot about the catacombs, and thick vegetation grew over the entrances, hiding them from view. It wasn't until the late 1500s that Antonio Bosio began the search and scientific exploration of the ancient catacombs. Most important is the irrefutable evidence the catacombs provide us today that early Christians believed, beyond a shadow of a doubt, that Jesus Christ rose from the dead. And the early Christians who existed so close to the time of Jesus were clearly in a good position to know the truth.

CONCLUSION

The people close to the time of the resurrection of Jesus had the greatest ability to judge the veracity of the historical accuracy of the event. Many eye-witnesses chose to honor Jesus and die to spread the gospel, rather than to bow down to some other "god." Historical and archaeological evidence supports the broadscale martyrdom. The fact that many early Christians in the best possible position to know the truth died to tell the story lends especially strong credibility to the fact that the crucifixion and resurrection of Jesus is true.

The Existence of the Christian Church

Chung Lou Lee's family excitedly awaited the arrival of American missionary Terri Blanchard, who had promised she would bring a Bible to their underground church near Beijing, China. Christianity was forbidden in the family's community, and Terri risked death if she were caught.

MUHAMMAD ABDILLAH AWOKE and began his morning devotions. He carefully pried the floorboards loose in his tiny shack to retrieve his Bible from its secret place. This morning, as every other for the past two years, his mind recalled one sickening, horrific day. It was a day he will never forget—when his brother Atullah was pulled from his home, tied to a stake, doused with gasoline, and burned alive—simply for worshiping Jesus.

THE SMITH FAMILY ROSE EARLY in Rose Hill, Mississippi, and like every Sunday drove to their tiny church. The children were placed in a Sunday school where they learned about Jesus in between pulling hair and rolling on the floor. The parents joined in worship with others, praising God and prayerfully thanking Jesus for the many blessings he had provided.

MR. ZIPPER, OF THE TINY SCHOOLHOUSE in Cowtown, Colorado, was teaching history to his fifth graders. He spoke about the Pilgrims and how they founded the United States for the freedom to worship as they wanted. There was no disputing that the early United States was founded on Christianity. It was a historical fact.

NOBODY DOUBTS THE EXISTENCE of the Christian church. Not only is it the largest religion in the world (some 33 percent of all the world's population claim to be Christian), but it has survived persecution ever since its founding shortly after the crucifixion of Jesus in about A.D. 33. Christianity exists in every corner of the world, even where it is strictly prohibited with the threat of death.

The World of Christianity

Today approximately one-third of the world claims to be Christian. In A.D. 33 (the estimated time of Jesus' death), the Jewish population is estimated to have been less than one-half of one percent of the world—a level that it still approximates.

Christianity started from this base of Jews. In fact, early on virtually *all* Christians were Jews. However, Christianity quickly spread to the Gentiles as well. As martyrdom took its toll and Christianity became *more removed in both time and geography from Palestine* at the time of Jesus, the percentage of Jews who were

Christian dropped, while the percentage of the world population who became Christian soared. Thus, the world's decision—with "votes being cast" by people's very lives—indicated that more people believed in the resurrection of Jesus than in the widely circulated story that his body was stolen by the disciples.

The Foundation of Christianity—the Resurrection

The foundation of the Christian church is the resurrection of Jesus Christ. The apostle Paul said: "And if Christ has not been raised, your faith is futile; you are still in your sins" (1 Corinthians 15:17). This is an extremely powerful fact. The Christian church is *not* a philosophical religion like Hinduism, Buddhism, or various New Age religions. Instead, the Christian church is tied to one overwhelmingly central issue—*that the resurrection of Jesus Christ is a historical fact!*

This is not to say that the resurrection of Jesus Christ is the *only* important theological issue in Christianity; far from it. The *crucifixion* of Jesus was the event that provided salvation (i.e., the sacrifice) for those who have a personal relationship with him. However, it was the *resurrection* of Jesus that verified his prophetic claim that he was the Son of God—the Messiah—and *that he would overcome death so that we might have eternal life.* Only God could achieve this resurrection. It was absolutely necessary for Jesus' promise of salvation to have any significance. No other religious leaders have done anything similar. The resurrection caused the early disciples to rejoice in knowing that Jesus was who he said he was and that eternal life was assured. The resurrection gave the disciples the confidence to joyfully face death knowing that a greater reward existed for them in heaven.

Because Christianity is based on a *historical event* that demonstrates the divinity of Jesus, it is very different than any other religion. Christianity can be tested and verified by that single historical event. If it occurred, then Jesus, in fact, is Lord and Savior. If not, he is not. The means of proving any such historical event is by "legal" proof, or proof by eyewitness testimony, and by other often circumstantial evidence.

As indicated already, there is vast eyewitness testimony that the resurrection occurred. It was provided by many witnesses, including the disciples who had a radical change in attitude as they became bold proponents of Christ immediately following the resurrection. The disciples and many others willingly gave their lives in order to spread the story of their testimony.

Overcoming a Theological Dilemma—One God or Three?

As a theocracy, the Jews took their religion very seriously. The laws of Moses (the first five books of the Bible) were well known. Included in this theological thinking was the importance of a single God, which was at odds with the polytheistic cultures of the time.

The teachings of Jesus spoke of the idea of a three-in-one God. Even with the last words he spoke before ascending into heaven, Jesus exhorted his disciples to baptize others in the name of the three-in-one God: "Therefore go and make disciples of all nations, baptizing them in the name of the *Father* and of the *Son* and of the *Holy Spirit*" (Matthew 28:19).

To the Jews, the idea of Jesus, as a man, being God while also praying to God the Father and teaching the existence of the Holy Spirit was confusing at a minimum and blasphemy at worst. In some people's eyes it would be like worshiping three separate gods, which is strictly forbidden by Mosaic Law. Therefore, any change in thinking to accept Jesus as part of God (along with the Holy Spirit) was a fundamental theological change that would have been difficult to do in such a serious theocracy. Yet it was a change required by Christianity.

When we consider the existence of the church in light of the conditions at the time, we should not only consider the difficulty of 1) the miracle of the resurrection itself and 2) the horror of the persecution, but we should also consider 3) *the theological difficulty of accepting the idea of the Trinity,* in which Jesus was God. The existence of the church shows that *the majority of the population overcame all three of these difficulties and believed in the historical resurrection!*

Again, what makes this so very important is that the essence of Christianity rests on the truth of this one historical event—an event that verified the deity of Jesus. No other religion has anything remotely like it. So strong was the conviction of early believers that they backed it up with their lives.

The History and Persecution of the Church

The history and persecution of the Christian church is well documented. We know that 3,000 people were added to the disciples of Jesus within days after the resurrection (see Acts 2:41). Peter, previously an inarticulate, somewhat timid fisherman, spoke boldly to a crowd of people immediately after the resurrection. His words had a profound impact on a city aware of the resurrection—in many cases due to eyewitness testimony. After addressing the crowd and describing what the crucifixion and resurrection were all about, he said to them:

> "Therefore let all Israel be assured of this: God has made this Jesus, whom you crucified, both Lord and Christ."
>
> When the people heard this, they were cut to the heart and said to Peter and the other apostles, "Brothers, what shall we do?"
>
> Peter replied, "Repent and be baptized, every one of you, in the name of Jesus Christ for the forgiveness of

your sins. And you will receive the gift of the Holy Spirit. The promise is for you and your children and for all who are far off—for all whom the Lord our God will call."

With many other words he warned them; and he pleaded with them, "Save yourselves from this corrupt generation." Those who accepted his message were baptized, and about three thousand were added to their number that day (Acts 2:36-41).

Shortly thereafter, we know that the number of people in the early church jumped to 5,000 men (Acts 4:4). Since it was normal at that time to count the men only, as the leaders of the household, and since the women and older children usually held the same belief, we can probably at least double this estimate of church size at that time. That would conservatively place the size of the church in Jerusalem between 10,000 and 15,000 people very shortly after the resurrection. The church continued to grow rapidly (Acts 5:14; 6:7).

I estimate that by the time Jerusalem fell in A.D. 70, about 70 percent of the city were followers of Jesus. This would place the number at about 70,000 people. When we consider that there were about 20,000 Christians (in Jerusalem) shortly after the resurrection, then that number does not seem odd at all. In fact, growth in Christianity would have only had to have averaged about 1.8 percent per year to reach that number. We know that in the first few years, it exploded far beyond that 1.8 percent per year.

Christians in and around Jerusalem were persecuted from the outset. Stephen is the first recorded Christian martyr. His martyrdom is estimated to have occurred in about A.D. 35, shortly after the resurrection. Stephen was the first of seven to be elected to be a deacon in the church, responsible for the distribution of alms. He was accused of blasphemy in much the same way as Jesus was—Stephen essentially confirmed Jesus as the Son of God, and worshiped him as such. The Bible describes how Stephen enflamed the religious leaders and the events that followed:

> "You stiff-necked people, with uncircumcised hearts and ears! You are just like your fathers: You always resist the Holy Spirit! Was there ever a prophet your fathers did not persecute? They even killed those who predicted the coming of the Righteous One. And now you have betrayed and murdered him—you who have received the law that was put into effect through angels but have not obeyed it."
>
> When they heard this, they were furious and gnashed their teeth at him. But Stephen, full of the Holy Spirit, looked up to heaven and saw the glory of God, and Jesus standing at the right hand of God. "Look," he said, "I see heaven open and the Son of Man standing at the right hand of God."
>
> At this they covered their ears and, yelling at the top of their voices, they all rushed at him, dragged him out of the city and began to stone him. Meanwhile, the witnesses laid their clothes at the feet of a young man named Saul.
>
> While they were stoning him, Stephen prayed, "Lord Jesus, receive my spirit." Then he fell on his knees and cried out, "Lord, do not hold this sin against them." When he had said this, he fell asleep (Acts 7:51-60).

This act of stoning Stephen was a violation of Roman law; the Roman authorities, alone, held the ultimate right to issue the death penalty.

The same Saul mentioned in this account of the martyrdom of Stephen, became known later in the Bible as Paul, and he was responsible for initiating the expansion of Christianity after he converted. He started by establishing a base of operation in Antioch (a city that is today located in Syria). From there he embarked on three major missionary journeys throughout Asia Minor and Macedonia (Greece). During these travels, many new churches were established.

Paul's first trip took him to Cyprus, then Asia Minor. He journeyed with Barnabas and John Mark (who failed to complete the trip) to the cities of Salamis, Paphos, Perga, Antioch in Pisidia, and Attalia.

On his next trip Paul traveled to both Asia Minor and Macedonia. During this journey, he worked with Silas and Timothy and set up churches in Philippi, Thessalonica, and Ephesus.

On Paul's third and final missionary journey, he worked with Apollos and others, and established new churches in Philippi and Corinth.

Throughout Paul's missionary days, up until the time of his own martyrdom, he communicated to the churches that he established through letters. These letters have become known as the "Pauline Epistles" and are now books of the New Testament—of which they make up about one third.

The persecution of Christianity outside of Jerusalem increased considerably under Nero, when in A.D. 64 he blamed the great fire of Rome on the Christians and initiated the first of many mass executions. Nero was ruthless. He made execution of Christians entertainment that was watched on a frequent basis by the citizens of Rome and elsewhere in the Roman Empire. Followers of Jesus were thrown to the lions, burned at the stake, impaled on spears and poles, and beheaded. Fear was widespread in the Christian community, although believers accepted their fate as martyrs with joy—as recorded in many historical writings. (Joy in suffering as their Savior did and in the knowledge that they would be with him in heaven.)

Instead of killing off the church as Nero intended, it actually flourished. As the prior chapter pointed out, persecution expanded after Nero: 1) Emperor Domitian ordering Christians to be brought to Roman tribunals to be questioned about their faith. 2) Trajan forcing Christians to renounce their faith by bowing down to statues of him. 3) Hadrian killing 10,000 Christians. 4) Hadrian also establishing pagan landmarks on the Christian holy sites and murdering Christians. The list goes on and on until Emperor Constantine stopped the persecution in A.D. 313. Thousands of Christians died because of belief in one historical fact—the resurrection.

So from the time of Jesus until A.D. 313, the Christian church flourished in spite of extreme persecution. These years would have probably been the easiest years for Christianity to disappear. Eyewitnesses would have all died, yet faith in Jesus continued more intensely than ever. In A.D. 303, an edict from Rome stated that anyone caught with sacred writings of the Christian church would be executed. Christianity had totally moved underground, but still it continued to grow.

Constantine made Christianity an acceptable religion of the Roman Empire. People in the empire were free to reject Christianity (they were just not permitted to persecute Christians any longer). In the years that followed, the church grew by leaps and bounds. The church at Rome became more prominent. Iranaeus of Lyon referred to the Roman church as preeminent in relation to other sister churches. In 1054, a division in thinking occurred between the Eastern church and the Roman church that resulted in the division of the Greek Orthodox branch of Christianity from Rome.

The Byzantine Period

The period from 324 to 1430 is generally referred to as the Byzantine period (broken down into early, middle, and late periods). It was a time when many Bibles were copied and distributed, and Christianity became embedded in artwork that would stand the test of time. The Byzantine period was a time of strong growth of the church, and Christianity became center stage among world religions. The belief in the resurrection was obviously very strong.

The Crusades

The "Christian" crusades started in 1096 and lasted until about 1300. Defined as several separate crusades (the first to the fifth and others), the stated intention was to liberate the holy lands from the barbarians who controlled them. The crusades, however, reflected anything but the beliefs of Christianity. Crusaders pillaged and murdered many innocent people, including Jews and Christians (this practice was condemned by the church). The intentions of the crusades failed miserably; however, the crusades did indicate a continuing strong belief in Christianity.

The Protestant and Catholic Reformations

In the early 1500s the Roman Catholic church was criticized for many abuses including the selling of indulgences ("tickets" to avoid the torture in "purgatory" after death), the selling of Church offices, and the proliferation of questionable religious practices and rituals. Initially led by Martin Luther, the Protestant movement eventually expanded and was accepted by King Henry VIII as the "official" religion of England (for political, not doctrinal reasons). The Roman Catholic Church, recognizing its problems, launched a counter reformation from 1545–1563 to extricate much nonbiblical doctrine from its teachings. The strength and belief in the resurrection and its importance continued to be evident. During this period, Christianity was revitalized.

The Christian Church Worldwide

Since the time of the reformation, the Christian church has continued to prosper in virtually every corner of the world, despite cruel treatment and martyrdom in some locations. Christianity was the reason for the English settlement of the United States and was its foundation for both religion and education in the nation's early years. Christianity continues to be spread worldwide by missionaries willing to die for their faith based on one simple, strong belief—the belief that Jesus Christ rose from the dead.

The resurrection of Jesus as a real, historical event has been the cornerstone of Christianity through the centuries. The fact that it has been believed by countless individuals in an unbroken string of generations has allowed little opportunity for sudden "Jesus" myths or legends. In addition, there is the ability to always contrast modern belief with thousands of ancient New Testament and non-Christian writings to compare consistency of various accounts and ensure historical accuracy in doctrine and beliefs.

Unlike other religions, Christianity is based on *historical fact*. It is not a faceless philosophy. If the resurrection of Jesus never happened, there would be absolutely no basis for the Christian church. It would not exist. As we've seen, there is a continuous history of the church without any break. One can go all the way back to the earliest church documents (early manuscripts of the New Testament) and find the essential dogma of the church unchanged.

The many martyrs of the Christian faith all died for essentially one thing—to defend the historical fact that Jesus Christ rose from the dead. Enemies of the church had hoped that execution of church leaders would quell the expansion of Christianity. Instead, it increased the resolve of Christians and provided provocative evidence of the historicity of the resurrection of Jesus to later generations.

CONCLUSION

The existence of the Christian church is undeniable. It exists solely on the basis of the broadscale belief in the historical event of the resurrection of Jesus Christ. If this resurrection did not take place historically, the Christian church would not have existed at the outset, nor would it exist today. It stands apart from any other religion in that *it depends upon one single historical, supernatural event for its existence—the resurrection of Jesus.*

The Church Fathers

Polycarp, the Bishop of Smyrna, paused in deep thought before he addressed the other church leaders. Their Lord, Jesus, had been resurrected just over 70 years ago, and the group of leaders had been using the Gospels and letters in teaching throughout the church. Since A.D. 64, Christian worship was held primarily in private homes due to persecution, and it was more important than ever to ensure consistency and accuracy of the story of Jesus and the teaching of the apostles.

"I encourage all of you to memorize as much of this inspired writing as possible," proclaimed Polycarp, "since as we speak today, there are those who would like to have the entire writings about Christ destroyed. Even as we meet, our dear friend Ignatius, Bishop of Antioch, is on his way to Rome to be executed. Let's not let his martyrdom be in vain as we continue to spread the Word with great zeal."

The year was A.D. 107.

IT DIDN'T TAKE LONG FOR THE EARLY CHURCH to commit the story of Jesus to writing. By A.D. 64 persecution was in full swing—only about 30 years after Jesus' death. And the Christian church was exploding, seemingly out of control to those wishing to quell it. Many scholars believe that three of the four gospels had been recorded by then in order to ensure that trustworthy, standardized accounts could be passed on to others. By the end of the first century, all of the Gospels, the book of Acts, the letters, and the book of Revelation—all of the books making up the New Testament—had been completed.

In addition to writing down the New Testament shortly after Jesus' death, the leaders of the first-century church (and in the beginning of the second century) committed large sections to memory. This memorization helped guard against errors since anyone wanting to intentionally distort the gospel message would have to contend with the memories of the church fathers as well.

Early church fathers also included verses and sections of the New Testament in other writings and teachings on a vast scale. Literally all books of the New Testament were cited! In fact, nearly every verse can be found in nonbiblical writings.

So extensive was this early recognition and reference to the New Testament, that scholars analyzing it proclaim that if all of the copies of the New Testament were destroyed it could be reconstructed solely from external references by others. The vast number of quotes by early church leaders is summarized below:[1]

Author	Dates	Gospel/Acts	Letters	Revelation	Total
Justin Martyr	133 A.D.	278	49	3	330
Irenaeus	125–202	1,232	522	65	1,819
Clement (Alex.)	150–212	1,061	1,334	11	2,406
Origen	185–253	9,580	8,177	165	17,922
Tertullian	160–220	4,324	2,729	205	7,258
Hippolytus	170–235	776	414	188	1,378
Eusebius	263–339	3,469	1,680	27	5,176
TOTAL		20,720	14,905	664	36,289

In addition to this list, the well-known martyr Ignatius (A.D. 70–110) in his seven epistles quoted from the books of Matthew, John, Acts, Romans, 1 Corinthians, Galatians, Ephesians, Philippians, Colossians, 1 and 2 Thessalonians, 1 and 2 Timothy, James, and 1 Peter. Ignatius was personally acquainted with some of the apostles and had every opportunity to verify the accuracy of the life of Jesus through the eyewitnesses themselves.

Early Church Baptism

Priscilla looked up at the priest with tears in her eyes as he asked the most important questions of her life, "Do you believe in God, the Father Almighty...in Jesus Christ, the Son of God, who was born of the Holy Spirit and the Virgin Mary...in the Holy Spirit, in the holy church, and the resurrection of the body?" Her husband and two young children looked on, with an approving smile.

"Yes I believe," she said, her voice deep with emotion.

With that Priscilla was dipped in water and then anointed with oil. "This I do as a sign of your baptism with the Holy Spirit," the priest continued. Overjoyed, Priscilla started weeping and tightly hugged her husband while thinking about her new relationship with the Lord Jesus Christ.

Only 180 years had passed since Jesus had walked the face of the earth.

The Early Church Creeds

An early church leader, Hippolytus, wrote about baptisms in the early 200s. The words selected as a statement of faith were foundational to what Jesus himself regarded as fundamental to Christian belief. We can be assured of this because those crafting such statements of faith were within a few generations of Jesus. The doctrine was discussed by Christian leaders such as Ignatius (A.D. 70–110) and Clement of Rome (A.D. 95), who both had actual contact with the apostles themselves. Ignatius and Clement then passed it on to other early leaders including Polycarp (70–156), Justin Martyr (c. 100–167), Irenaeus (125–202), Tertullian (160–220), and Hippolytus (170–235).

There was unbroken continuity between the teachings of Jesus and the apostles and the Christian church's defined statements of faith.

The Apostles' Creed, which is a fundamental statement of faith actively used by many denominations today, is believed to have its roots in the *Interrogatory Creed of Hippolytus* (c. A.D. 215). The Apostles' Creed is especially significant because it affirms:

- Jesus' "oneness" with God; the Creator of the universe

- Jesus' virgin birth

- Jesus' bodily resurrection

- The triune nature of God (Father, Son, and Holy Spirit)

- The forgiveness of sin

The Apostles' Creed was specifically intended to combat Gnosticism—the heretical belief of opposing spiritual realms of good and evil, with the material world aligned with evil. Gnosticism was philosophical in origin, and it rejected the redemption and bodily resurrection of Jesus.

The Apostles' Creed

I believe in God, the Father Almighty,
    the Creator of heaven and earth,
    and in Jesus Christ, His only Son, our Lord:
Who was conceived of the Holy Spirit,
    born of the Virgin Mary,
    suffered under Pontius Pilate,
    was crucified, died, and was buried.
He descended into hell.
The third day He arose again from the dead.
He ascended into heaven
    and sits at the right hand of God the Father Almighty,
    whence He shall come to judge the living and the dead.
I believe in the Holy Spirit, the holy catholic church,
    the communion of saints,
    the forgiveness of sins,
    the resurrection of the body,
    and life everlasting.
Amen.

Another early creed of significance was the Nicene Creed adapted about A.D. 325 (later revised by the First Council of

Constantinople, 381). This creed was developed at the First Council of Nicaea, convened by Roman Emperor Constantine. The creed's purpose was to counter the heresy of Arianism, which rejected the deity of Jesus.

THE NICENE CREED

We believe in one God,
    the Father, the Almighty,
    maker of heaven and earth,
    of all that is, seen and unseen.

We believe in one Lord, Jesus Christ,
    the only Son of God,
    eternally begotten of the Father,
    God from God, Light from Light,
    true God from true God,
    begotten, not made,
    of one Being with the Father.
    Through him all things were made.
    For us and for our salvation
        he came down from heaven:
    by the power of the Holy Spirit
        he became incarnate from the Virgin Mary,
        and was made man.
    For our sake he was crucified under Pontius Pilate;
        he suffered death and was buried.
        On the third day he rose again
            in accordance with the Scriptures;
        he ascended into heaven
            and is seated at the right hand of the Father.
He will come again in glory to judge the living and the dead,
    and his kingdom will have no end.

We believe in the Holy Spirit, the Lord, the giver of life,
    who proceeds from the Father and the Son.
    With the Father and the Son he is worshiped and glorified.
    He has spoken through the Prophets.
    We believe in one holy catholic and apostolic Church.
    We acknowledge one baptism for the forgiveness of sins.
    We look for the resurrection of the dead,
        and the life of the world to come.   Amen.

Finally, the Athanasian Creed was adapted in the early 300s (originally ascribed to Saint Athanasius, but now believed to be from an unknown author). The purpose of this creed was to define the doctrine of the trinity and the bodily incarnation of Jesus.

The Athanasian Creed

Whoever wants to be saved should above all cling to the catholic faith.

Whoever does not guard it whole and inviolable will doubtless perish eternally.

Now this is the catholic faith: We worship one God in trinity and the Trinity in unity, neither confusing the persons nor dividing the divine being.

For the Father is one person, the Son is another, and the Spirit is still another.

But the deity of the Father, Son, and Holy Spirit is one, equal in glory, coeternal in majesty.

What the Father is, the Son is, and so is the Holy Spirit.

Uncreated is the Father; uncreated is the Son; uncreated is the Spirit.

The Father is infinite; the Son is infinite; the Holy Spirit is infinite.

Eternal is the Father; eternal is the Son; eternal is the Spirit:

And yet there are not three eternal beings, but one who is eternal;

as there are not three uncreated and unlimited beings, but one who is uncreated and unlimited.

Almighty is the Father; almighty is the Son; almighty is the Spirit:

And yet there are not three almighty beings, but one who is almighty.

Thus the Father is God; the Son is God; the Holy Spirit is God:

And yet there are not three gods, but one God.

Thus the Father is Lord; the Son is Lord; the Holy Spirit is Lord:

And yet there are not three lords, but one Lord.

As Christian truth compels us to acknowledge each distinct person as God and Lord, so catholic religion forbids us to say that there are three gods or lords.

The Father was neither made nor created nor begotten;

the Son was neither made nor created, but was alone begotten of the Father;

the Spirit was neither made nor created, but is proceeding from the Father and the Son.

Thus there is one Father, not three fathers; one Son, not three sons; one Holy Spirit, not three spirits.

And in this Trinity, no one is before or after, greater or less than the other;

but all three persons are in themselves, coeternal and coequal; and so we must worship the Trinity in unity and the one God in three persons.

Whoever wants to be saved should think thus about the Trinity.

It is necessary for eternal salvation that one also faithfully believe that our Lord Jesus Christ became flesh.

For this is the true faith that we believe and confess: That our Lord Jesus Christ, God's Son, is both God and man.

He is God, begotten before all worlds from the being of the Father, and he is man, born in the world from the being of his mother—

existing fully as God, and fully as man with a rational soul and a human body;

equal to the Father in divinity, subordinate to the Father in humanity.

Although he is God and man, he is not divided, but is one Christ.

He is united because God has taken humanity into himself; he does not transform deity into humanity.

He is completely one in the unity of his person, without confusing his natures.

For as the rational soul and body are one person, so the one Christ is God and man.

He suffered death for our salvation.

He descended into hell and rose again from the dead.

He ascended into heaven and is seated at the right hand of the Father.

He will come again to judge the living and the dead.

At his coming all people shall rise bodily to give an account of their own deeds.

Those who have done good will enter eternal life,

those who have done evil will enter eternal fire.

This is the catholic faith.

One cannot be saved without believing this firmly and faithfully.

The New Testament Canon

"Canon" simply means "standardized." In biblical understanding, it has the special importance of implying Scripture is from God, or "God-breathed." There is substantial evidence from historical writings that indicates the canon of the Old Testament was essentially "closed" (determined) no later than 167 B.C. Jesus referred frequently to the Scriptures as if they were a preordained collection of words from God. No room for variance was ever suggested. The Old Testament canon was officially approved by the Jews in A.D. 70.

The Christian church had essentially determined a canon (an accepted collection of books) for the entire Bible by A.D. 200. Early church fathers Irenaeus (C. A.D. 130) and Origen (C. A.D. 180) both listed all 27 books of the New Testament (although some were listed as suspect: 6 by Irenaeus, and 5 by Origen).[2] However, final confirmation of the canon did not occur until the Council of Carthage in A.D. 397.

It is significant that the canon was scrutinized shortly after the time of the writing of the books of the New Testament and remained under scrutiny for many years before its final approval. This way, the books of the New Testament had substantial time for critics to voice potential concerns and for those who had the best, closest knowledge to review them.

Jesus Confirmed the Gospel

Jesus actually preconfirmed the development of the New Testament and its inspiration by the Holy Spirit. While on earth, Jesus gave the apostles the authority to write it. He then further prophesied and confirmed it.

First, authority was granted. The Holy Spirit was to guide the very words of the apostles:

But the Counselor, the Holy Spirit, whom the Father will send in my name, will teach you all things and will remind you of everything I have said to you (John 14:26).

But when he, the Spirit of truth, comes, he will guide you into all truth. He will not speak on his own; he will speak only what he hears, and he will tell you what is yet to come (John 16:13-14).

For the Holy Spirit will teach you at that time what you should say (Luke 12:12).

Second, the gospel was prophesied—17 times Jesus prophesied that the apostles would provide the gospel. Examples include:

And this gospel of the kingdom will be preached in the whole world as a testimony to all nations, and then the end will come (Matthew 24:14).

I tell you the truth, wherever this gospel is preached throughout the world, what she has done will also be told, in memory of her (Matthew 26:13).

For whoever wants to save his life will lose it, but whoever loses his life for me and for the gospel will save it (Mark 8:35).

Heaven and earth will pass away, but my words will never pass away (Luke 21:33).

Third, Jesus confirmed the gospel during the period in which it was being preached on three separate occasions:

One night the Lord spoke to Paul in a vision: "Do not be afraid; keep on speaking, do not be silent" (Acts 18:9).

> I fell into a trance and saw the Lord speaking. "Quick!" he said to me. "Leave Jerusalem immediately, because they will not accept your testimony about me" (Acts 22:18).

> The following night the Lord stood near Paul and said, "Take courage! As you have testified about me in Jerusalem, so you must also testify in Rome" (Acts 23:11).

While the New Testament was written after the extensive appearance of Jesus on earth prior to the resurrection, we find that Jesus foretold of its coming. Furthermore, he confirmed the writing of the New Testament during the period in which it was being told and later compiled.

Knowing that the Holy Spirit guided the writing of the New Testament, and knowing that Jesus himself foretold and confirmed it, we can be confident in its words.

CONCLUSION

The early church fathers were deeply interested in the gospel of Jesus Christ as well as in the other portions of the New Testament. Large portions of the New Testament were committed to memory and were written in nonbiblical sources. The fact that virtually the entire New Testament can be reconstructed from these extrabiblical sources is indicative of the extent to which it was being read and the extent to which it was believed. Belief in the words of the New Testament message is, of course, tantamount to belief in Jesus.

Evidence from Early Manuscripts

A tuero looked carefully down each long corridor before knocking on the door.

Tichus opened the door slightly. "Is it safe?" he asked.

"Yes," replied Atuero, his voice cracking with obvious emotion as he was quickly whisked inside. "Did you hear about Jonas?" asked Atuero, his hands trembling as he fought to catch his breath.

"No," said Tichus. "What about him?"

"They killed him!" cried Atuero. "They killed him!" he said as he began to sob uncontrollably.

"How did it happen?" asked Tichus.

"He was caught last night along the esplanade with four codices. They threw him on the ground and beat him into a bloody mess. This morning after one of those mock trials, they paraded him into the center of town, tied him to a post, and lit him on fire in front of his wife and three little children. It was awful! Simply awful!"

Atuero was distraught with emotion and tears were streaming down his face. Tichus reached out and drew Atuero close to comfort him. "Well, just remember, he's with the Lord now. We need to be strong—even more so than ever."

By now the other four men who had been working upstairs came down to see what the commotion was all about. After hearing the story they decided the best thing they could do was to return to the upper room and redouble their efforts to make more copies of the writings of the apostles.

Members of the church of Ephesus that had been established only a few years ago by Paul of Tarsus, the men were a dedicated team whose purpose, like many other church groups throughout the region, was to make duplicates of the writings of the apostles and pass them on to people who did not have a chance to hear the story of Jesus. It was a very risky undertaking, as the Roman soldiers had been told to seek out and kill anyone involved in such work. But it was also rewarding. Atuero, Tichus, and the others spent the morning in prayer for the family of Jonas, and for the success and safety of their efforts. They realized that their sacrifice could provide eternal salvation for many in the region, and perhaps even others in years to come.

THE EARLY CHRISTIAN CHURCH EXPLODED onto the scene more quickly than any major theological or philosophical dogma before or since. The Bible indicates that about 3,000 were added to the group of believers on a single day—50 days after the resurrection (on the day now known as Pentecost). Presumably these were all men, since that is the way "people" were counted at the time. Adding woman, children, and existing believers, this would have brought the total number to approximately 6,000 to 10,000. A few days later when Peter and John were seized by the temple guard and placed in jail for preaching about the resurrection of Jesus (Acts 4:1-4), the number of Christians grew to about 5,000 men. Again, adding woman and children, this would have equated to perhaps 10,000 to 15,000 within days of the resurrection!

The rapid chain-reaction-type expansion of the church required some controls to ensure accuracy and consistency of the message. For that reason, the account of the ministry of Jesus and his death and resurrection was recorded by several different authors. Most scholars believe that Mark was the first Gospel (written A.D. 55–65),[1] since a considerable number of verses from Mark also exist in Matthew and Luke. Most scholars believe that a second, as yet undiscovered gospel designated "Q" was also written about that time, which contained the verses common in Matthew and Luke, but not in Mark. Luke is believed to have been written in the early 60s and Matthew sometime in the 70s. John was believed to be the latest Gospel of all, written perhaps to "fill in" important elements not recorded in the earlier Gospels. Scholars believe it was written sometime after A.D. 80.

In addition to recording accurate accounts of Jesus for distribution in a rapidly expanding church, it was also necessary to provide guidance and organization for growth. The letters of Paul were designed for such a purpose. Like the Gospels, they were widely copied and distributed. *The Gospels, the letters and the book of Revelation* (all of the New Testament) *were accepted by many people as inspired by God* at the time of the writing of the autographs. The church fathers had agreed on the writings of the New Testament by the early 200s, and it was officially canonized in 397.

The *Old Testament* of the Bible was copied for centuries by trained scribes, with detailed scriptural copy rules that resulted in precision recording without error (see the Dead Sea Scrolls, pages 192-195). This was not the case with *New Testament* copies that, for the most part, were *not* made by trained scribes, but instead by educated people whose purpose was to perpetuate the gospel message and church instruction in the face of extensive persecution. In a sense, it was a race against time. Could an adequate number of copies be made and distributed in time to replace those being destroyed by the Romans and Jewish religious leaders? Because the copying of the New Testament was not in the tightly controlled environment of the Old Testament, some copies did contain slight variations. However, the variances are not significant, and when the vast quantity of manuscripts is viewed as a whole, it is easy to corroborate the accuracy of the text.

Ancient New Testament Manuscripts

Today, nearly 2,000 years since the time of Jesus, we have an extraordinary number of ancient manuscripts still in existence for the New Testament. This is truly remarkable in the face of early persecution that sought to destroy the New Testament records. These copies exist in several forms and languages:[2]

Extant Manuscripts	Number in Existence
Greek	5,664
Latin Vulgate	8,000–10,000
Ethiopic, Slavic, Armenian	8,000
Other	about 1,000
TOTAL	about 24,000

Also important is the proximity of New Testament records to the resurrection—the earliest of which are even within the time of the eyewitnesses. Many more are within a generation or two. Two important criteria help to ensure the content of the text: 1) a large number of consistent manuscripts, and 2) the dating of early manuscripts in close proximity to the events. This compares very favorably to other ancient documents that we casually regard as history:[3]

Author and Ancient Document	Number of Manuscripts	Proximity to Autograph of Earliest Copy (years)
Homer's *Iliad*	643	400
Herodotus — History	8	1,350
Thucydides — History	8	1,300
Plato	7	1,300
Demonsthenes	200	1,400
Caesar — Gallic Wars	10	1,000
Livy — History of Rome	1 partial, 19 copies	400 1,000
Tacitus — Annals	20	1,000
Pliny Secundus — History	7	750
New Testament	5,366	50–225 years

It is apparent that the New Testament stands head and shoulders above all other major books of antiquity in both the categories of 1) number of corroboratory copies and 2) the proximity of the copies to the original writing. This is of great significance. We readily accept other books of history written by such authors as Julius Caesar, Herodotus, Thucydides, Livy, and Tacitus even though documentary confirmation is far less in number, and copies are much further removed from the original autographs. We should have significantly greater confidence in the accuracy of the transmission over time of the New Testament.

Finally, regarding the consistency of the vast number of New Testament copies themselves, we find substantial agreement and no doctrinal disagreement. As mentioned, New Testament copyists for the most part were not scribes trained in the classical sense. An example of a meaningless inconsistency between two New Testament documents might be transposition of word order. In English, it makes a great deal of difference if we write "man eats chicken" or "chicken eats man." In Greek it does not. Each sentence in Greek has a defined subject, verb, and predicate; hence the order of words makes no difference.[4] Biblical scholars who have analyzed New Testament documentation proclaim it far "purer" than any other book of antiquity. Scholars Norman Geisler and William Nix conclude that the New Testament has survived in a "form that is 99.5% pure."[5]

The John Rylands Papyri

John 18:31-33, and also John 18:37-38, appear on what is known as the John Rylands Papyri:

> Pilate said, "Take him yourselves and judge him by your own law."
>
> "But we have no right to execute anyone," the Jews objected. This happened so that the words Jesus had spoken indicating the kind of death he was going to die would be fulfilled.
>
> Pilate then went back inside the palace, summoned Jesus and asked him, "Are you the king of the Jews?" (John 18:31-33).

"You are a king, then!" said Pilate.

Jesus answered, "You are right in saying I am a king. In fact, for this reason I was born, and for this I came into the world, to testify to the truth. Everyone on the side of truth listens to me."

"What is truth?" Pilate asked. With this he went out again to the Jews and said, "I find no basis for a charge against him" (John 18:37-38).

The John Rylands Papyri, dated back to A.D. 125, is the oldest known commonly accepted fragment of the New Testament in existence today. (*Note:* Although some scholars believe portions of the New Testament have been found in the Dead Sea Scrolls, others believe such finds are merely from the nonbiblical book of Enoch.)

The Rylands Papyri is important in its dating and location. Found in Egypt—hundreds of miles from the suspected place of the autograph in Asia Minor—it seems to indicate the original Gospel of John may well have been written as early as the forties.[6] The famous biblical scholar, F.F. Bruce, who was Ryland's professor at the University of Manchester, claims that the Gospel of John—the latest of the Gospels—was written in A.D. 90.[7]

Whether the original Gospel of John was written as early as the 40s or as late as A.D. 90, we know that it was present at the time of many eyewitnesses to the crucifixion and resurrection of Jesus. This provides assurance that it was available for examination regarding accuracy.

The Codex Sinaiticus

The Codex Sinaiticus is one of the most important ancient biblical manuscripts ever found because it is one of the earliest nearly complete copies of the Bible. Even the story of the discovery of the codex is interesting:

The fire burned warmly casting flickering shadows off the walls of the monastery at the base of Mount Sinai. The monks huddled around it in quiet conversation about the day's events. A young man of 30, Tischendorf from the University of Leipzig had arrived early in the day in search of manuscripts of the Bible. The monks were fascinated by his enthusiasm yet smiled privately wondering why finding old Bibles mattered so much to him.

Tischendorf was near the fire and reached over to a waste basket full of paper used to keep the fire going. As he was about to toss a sheet into the blaze, he stopped in disbelief at what he was holding in his hand. To his amazement, it was part of an ancient copy of the Septuagint version of the Bible. The monks laughed when Tischendorf told them what he had found, saying that they had already burned two waste baskets full of the same manuscript. The young man begged them to give him any other sheets of the manuscript, and asked them not to burn any others that they may have.

Tischendorf returned to his home and had the portions of the Bible he had retrieved published, naming them the codex Frederico-Augustanus. Later he returned a second time to the monastery and later yet a third time. By now he had gained the confidence and friendship of the monks. He brought a copy of a published version of the Septuagint, which he gave to the steward of the monastery. Later that evening the steward pulled Tischendorf aside.

"I have something to show you," he said as he reached into his closet and pulled out a manuscript that was meticulously wrapped in a red cloth. Slowly he opened it. Tischendorf couldn't believe his eyes. It was a nearly complete Bible, obviously of ancient origin. Tears streamed down his face. That evening,

Tischedorf stayed up all night pouring over the words of the manuscript. He wrote in his journal at the time, "it really seemed a sacrilege to sleep." Something truly important had been discovered.

Dr. Constantin Von Tischendorf's discovery of the manuscript, now known as Codex Sinaiticus, was made in 1859. It contains nearly all of the New Testament and over half of the Old Testament. The manuscript was eventually presented by the monastery to the Russian czar, and later bought by the British government for 100,000 pounds on Christmas Day in 1933.

The codex, written in Greek, was copied primarily from a master scroll sometime around A.D. 350. Experts have concluded that three scribes were involved in the writing, and as many as nine "correctors" had made some notations over the centuries. The codex consists of 148 14" x 15" pages written in brown ink in four columns, 48 lines per column, per page. It is consistent with the many early copies of portions of the New Testament that have been found (some of these portions of the Bible date back to the early second century). Today Codex Sinaiticus resides in the British Museum.

The Codex Sinaiticus, written only a few generations after the eyewitnesses of Jesus, provides corroboration that the text of the New Testament is an accurate representation Jesus' life, death, and resurrection.

Codex Vaticanus

According to famous author and historian Eusebius, Constantine requested 50 "official" copies of the Bible be made to be held by Rome in the early 300s. Some scholars contend that the Codex Vaticanus, which has been held for centuries at the Vatican in Rome, is one of the actual 50 copies requested by Constantine.

Of this we can't be certain. We can be sure, however, of the importance of the manuscript due to its early origin and completeness.

Codex Vaticanus was written about A.D. 325. It is a nearly complete edition of today's Bible. It contains all of the Old Testament except for most of the book of Genesis. It contains the New Testament including the Gospels, Acts, and the Pauline letters through a portion of Hebrews. The pastoral letters and the book of Revelation are missing. The missing portion (most of Genesis and the end of the Bible) is because both the beginning and the end of the Bible had been damaged and were lost.

The Codex Vaticanus was written in Greek uncial—meaning in all capital letters with no punctuation. The Old Testament consists of 617 leaves (pages) and the New Testament consists of 142. Each leaf is about 11″ by 11″, and is formatted with three columns of 40, 44 lines per column. Scholars believe one scribe copied the Old Testament from a master, and another copied the New Testament likewise. One "corrector" is believed to have worked on the manuscript shortly after its writing and a second one hundreds of years later—probably about the tenth or eleventh century.

The significance of Codex Vaticanus is enormous. It is the earliest, nearly complete Bible we have available today, and it was written only 250 years after the time of the apostles. It is identical to the Bible we read today, with only a few exceptions that are often noted in many study Bibles.

Codex Vaticanus provides evidence that the story of Jesus as we read it today is identical to the beliefs that were widely accepted near the time of Jesus.

CONCLUSION

In terms of sheer numbers alone that allow for comparison of accuracy of copies, the New Testament is far above any ancient works that we commonly regard as history. Furthermore, the short time period between the autographs and the earliest extant copies provide great assurance of reliability. We can trust that the New Testament accounts of Jesus are accurate in that many consistent accounts were circulated within a few generations of the eyewitnesses to Jesus' life.

Evidence from Non-Christian Sources

The sun was setting and the cool dry air was blowing in over the Nile. The men carried their precious treasure with them to hide for safekeeping for future generations. Finally they reached the place where the documents would be safe. It was the east bank of the Nile. Cliffs towered above. The heavy jar they carried contained 45 texts in 13 papyrus books (codices), most of which were Gnostic writings (a copy of Plato's *Republic* was also included). The books were carefully packaged in jars, protected with "packing material" and topped with a bowl. Slowly, the jar was lowered into the hole, was covered with dirt, and a boulder was placed on top. Constantine had recently made Christianity the prominent religion of the Roman Empire. Now, the basics of Gnosticism would be preserved despite any persecution that might occur as a result of its being regarded as heretical by the leaders of the Christian church.

THE "GOSPEL OF THOMAS" WAS AMONG the documents that were discovered buried beneath a boulder in a large jar at the base of the cliffs on the east side of the Nile River in Egypt. This important discovery was made in 1945. Although the document bears the name "gospel," it is not canonical, nor is it even consistent with New Testament biblical teaching. The importance of the document is strictly as one of several nonbiblical sources that corroborate the existence and the words of Jesus.

Scholars consistently believe that the Gospel of Thomas was written sometime in the early to mid-second century. The most commonly cited date is c. A.D. 140. Essentially, it is supposedly an anthology of 114 obscure sayings of Jesus, which the prologue states were collected and transmitted by St. Didymus Jude Thomas. It was written in Coptic—which is Egyptian writing with an expanded Greek alphabet. Although a heretical source, the following list of parallels between the New Testament Gospels and the Gospel of Thomas (GTh) helps corroborate the existence of the widespread teachings of Jesus.

Matthew 5.10 — GTh 69a	Matthew 18.20 — GTh 30
Matthew 5.14 — GTh 32	Matthew 23.13 — GTh 39, 102
Matthew 6.2-4 — GTh 6,14	Luke 11.27-28 + 23:29 — GTh 79
Matthew 6.3 — GTh 62	Luke 12.13-14 — GTh 72
Matthew 7.6 — GTh 93	Luke 12.16-21 — GTh 63
Matthew 10.16 — GTh 39	Luke 12.49 — GTh 10
Matthew 11.30 — GTh 90	Luke 17.20-21 — GTh 3
Matthew 13.24-30 — GTh 57	John 1.9 — GTh 24
Matthew 13.44 — GTh 109	John 1.14 — GTh 28
Matthew 13.45-46 — GTh 76	John 4.13-15 — GTh 13
Matthew 13.47-50 — GTh 8	John 7.32-36 — GTh 38
Matthew 15.13 — GTh 40	John 8.12; 9.5 — GTh 77

The Gospel of Thomas clearly contradicts biblical teaching in important areas. It does not include any of Jesus' words regarding salvation or the ultimate historical revelation with the second coming of Jesus and creation of a "new heaven and a new earth" (salvation for the Gnostic is through self-knowledge).

Although found in Egypt, the Gospel of Thomas has also been found in Syria. At this point we can't be certain where it originated, nor where it may have been more popular.

Although the Gospel of Thomas has no canonical theological value and is from a sect regarded as heretical, the Gospel of Thomas does have historical value as a corroborative document that was written by those familiar with the teaching of Jesus, near the time of Jesus. It also supports much, although certainly not all, of the teaching of the New Testament.

References to Jesus in the Jewish Talmud

The Babylonian Talmud consists of 63 books of legal, ethical, spiritual, theological, ritual, and historical insight. Written and edited over many centuries, the part of the Talmud of most interest regarding Jesus is that portion that was written during the Tannaitic Period, from A.D. 70–200. A particularly significant text is in Sanhedrin 43a:

> On the eve of Passover they hanged Yeshu* [Jesus]. And an announcer went out in front of him for forty days, saying: "He is going to be stoned, because he practised sorcery and enticed and led Israel astray. Anyone who knows anything in his favor, let him come and plead in his behalf." But not having found any-thing in his favor, they hanged him on the eve of Passover.[1]

---

* One version of this text actually says "Yeshu the Nazarene."

This passage is important in that it was written by Jews that not only denied Jesus, but actively were proselytizing against him. Courts of law have long maintained that some of the most powerful testimony is corroborative testimony from hostile witnesses (in this case Jews testifying about Jesus). What can be deduced from the Talmud's writing are:

1. that Jesus existed

2. that Jesus was crucified (i.e., hanged) on the eve of Passover

3. that he performed miracles (the Jews referred to this as sorcery)

4. that Jesus led many people away from "legalistic Jewish teaching" (as indicated in the New Testament—Matthew 15:3-9)

5. that the Jewish leaders were plotting to kill Jesus

In summary, the evidence of Jesus written in the Talmud, by the very Jews who despised him, is strong testimony of his existence and acts. It is very significant that it is in total agreement with the account of Jesus in the New Testament, including references to miracles, to the crucifixion, and to other details.

References to Jesus by the Jewish Historian Josephus

Flavius Josephus is widely recognized as one of the greatest first-century historians. He, himself, has a colorful history.

Born in A.D. 37, only a few years after Jesus, he spent his youth in Israel. During his early 20s he was sent to Rome to negotiate the release of several priests held hostage by Emperor Nero. Upon returning home, the Jewish revolution had begun. Josephus was drafted into becoming the commander of the revolutionary force in Galilee. When the Roman general Vespasian captured the city of Jotapata, he found Josephus alone, with his group of followers all dead. At Josephus' direction, they had made a suicide pact, and oddly enough only Josephus did not take the deadly poison. Josephus proclaimed himself a prophet. Because Josephus flattered Vespasian into thinking that Vespasian was the messiah the Scriptures talked about, Vespasian spared Josephus' life. Later, when Vespasian became emperor of Rome, Josephus was brought into the royal family of the Flavians. For the remainder of the war, Josephus assisted the Roman commander Titus due to Josephus' knowledge of the Jewish culture. However, since Jerusalem regarded Josephus as a traitor, he had no luck in negotiating with the revolutionaries and, instead, became a witness to the destruction of Jerusalem and the Temple.

Josephus began writing the history of the war between the Romans and the Jews in the 70s. The book was apparently factually correct; however, it also was written to flatter the Romans and warn other provinces of the folly of opposing Rome. Later Josephus wrote a massive work about the history of the Jews *(Jewish Antiquities)*, which was published in A.D. 93/94.[2]

Josephus wrote about Jesus in his *Antiquities* as follows:

> Now there was about this time Jesus, a wise man IF IT BE LAWFUL TO CALL HIM A MAN, for he was a doer of wonders, A TEACHER OF SUCH MEN AS RECEIVE THE TRUTH WITH PLEASURE. He drew many after him BOTH OF THE JEWS AND THE GENTILES. HE WAS THE CHRIST. When Pilate, at the suggestion of the principal men among us, had condemned him to the cross, those that loved him at the first did not forsake him, FOR HE APPEARED TO THEM ALIVE AGAIN THE THIRD DAY, AS THE DIVINE PROPHETS HAD FORETOLD THESE AND TEN THOUSAND OTHER WONDERFUL THINGS ABOUT HIM, and the tribe of Christians, so named from him, are not extinct at this day (*Antiquities* 18:63-64).[3]

This writing is an extremely powerful statement by a non-Christian writing within the period of the eyewitnesses. Although there is some doubt regarding all of the words—some of which are believed to have been added (those in small caps are in question)—even if we consider only the words regarded by scholars as historically certain, we find corroboration of the historicity of Jesus, his miracles, his loyal followers, and his crucifixion by Pilate.

References to Jesus by the Historian Tacitus

Born only 22 years after the death of Jesus, Cornelius Tacitus was an energetic substitute consul and later proconsul in Asia Minor. Little is known about his life, but he was friends with the Roman consul Pliny the Younger.

Tacitus was known to be an eloquent, effective speaker. He tended to encourage his audiences to maintain a high moral ground. In his governing roles, he at times was in charge of government policy and even the army.

Tacitus is most famous for his important historical works, written at a time when very little history has survived. He wrote five *Histories*, of which four have survived (and part of the fifth). *Histories* covers only the history of Galba (A.D. 68–69) and the beginning of the reign of Vespasian (A.D. 70). He also wrote a 12-volume set called the *Annals,* which spans the historical period from the reign of Tiberius (from a point predating the ministry of Jesus) to the reigns of Claudius and the beginning of Nero (the last years of Paul's ministry). Writing in c. A.D. 115, Tacitus states in his *Annals* 15.44:

> But not all the relief that could come from man,
> not all the bounties that the prince could bestow, nor all
> the atonements which could be presented to the gods,
> availed to relieve Nero from the infamy of being
> believed to have ordered the conflagration of the fire of

Rome. Hence to suppress the rumor, he falsely charged with the guilt, and punished *Christians,* who were hated for their enormities. *Christus,* the founder of the name, was put to death by Pontius Pilate, procurator of Judea in the reign of Tiberius: but the *pernicious superstition,* repressed for a time broke out again, not only through Judea, where the mischief originated, but through the city of Rome also, where all things hideous and shameful from every part of the world find their center and become popular. Accordingly, an arrest was first made of all who pleaded guilty; then, upon their information, an immense multitude was convicted, not so much of the crime of firing the city, as of hatred against mankind.[4]

It is very significant that Tacitus, who was clearly anti-Christian, treated the existence of Jesus and his many believers in a matter-of-fact way. In addition, he indicated the belief the early Christians had in the resurrection (i.e., the "novel superstition"), and also provided extrabiblical support of many other details of the account in the New Testament writings.

Reference to Jesus by Historian Pliny the Younger

Pliny the Younger began practicing law in A.D. 79 at the age of 18. He very quickly developed a stellar reputation in civil law that led to demand for his services in political courts that tried officials for extortion. Major victories that stand out as indications of Pliny the Younger's skill included the condemnation of a governor of Africa, and also of a group of officials in Spain.[5]

Pliny the Younger was also an avid writer. He published ten major books containing a variety of letters. The letters were quite diverse in content. Many contained historical information relating to Pliny the Younger's relationship with people such as

Emperor Trajan. Yet others contain advice to young men, letters of inquiry, and descriptions of various settings of natural beauty.

Pliny the Younger's letters mark the first time the Roman government recognized Christianity as separate from Judaism. As governor of Bithynia (in Asia Minor), Pliny the Younger was caught in what seemed to be a quandary. Christians who were brought before him seemed to be harmless, yet were refusing to worship the Roman emperor (the Roman population generally regarded emperors as gods) and were harming the local idol trade because of their denunciation of idols. Pliny the Younger decided to execute several Christians who were brought before him if they did not recant their faith. Unsure of his action, he wrote to his friend Emperor Trajan for advice:

> Sir,
>
> It is my constant method to apply myself to you for the resolution of all my doubts; for who can better govern my dilatory way of proceeding or instruct my ignorance? I have never been present at the examination of the Christians [by others], on which account I am unacquainted with what uses to be inquired into, and what, and how far they used to be punished; nor are my doubts small, whether there be not a distinction to be made between the ages [of the accused]? And whether tender youth ought to have the same punishment with strong men? Whether there be not room for pardon upon repentance?" or whether it may not be an advantage to one that had been a Christian, that he has forsaken Christianity? Whether the bare name, without any crimes besides, or the crimes adhering to that name, be to be punished?
>
> In the meantime, I have taken this course about those who have been brought before me as Christians. I asked them whether they were Christians or not? If they

confessed that they were Christians, I asked them again, and a third time intermixing threatenings with the questions. If they persevered in their confession, I ordered them to be executed; for I did not doubt but, let their confession be of any sort whatsoever, this positiveness and inflexible obstinacy deserved to be punished.

There have been some of this mad sect whom I took notice of in particular as Roman citizens, that they might be sent to that city. After some time, as is usual in such examinations, the crime spread itself and many more cases came before me. A libel was sent to me, though without an author, containing many names [of persons accused]. These denied that they were Christians now, or ever had been. They called upon the gods, and supplicated to your image, which I caused to be brought to me for that purpose, with frankincense and wine; they also cursed Christ; none of which things, it is said, can any of those that are ready Christians be compelled to do; so I thought fit to let them go. Others of them that were named in the libel, said they were Christians, but presently denied it again; that indeed they had been Christians, but had ceased to be so, some three years, some many more and one there was that said he had not been so these twenty years. All these worshipped your image, and the images of our gods; these also cursed Christ. However, they assured me that the main of their fault, or of their mistake was this:—That they were wont, on a stated day, to meet together before it was light, and to sing a hymn to Christ, as to a god, alternately; and to oblige themselves by a sacrament [or oath], not to do anything that was ill: but that they would commit no theft, or pilfering, or adultery; that they would not break their promises, or deny what was deposited with them, when it was required back again; after which it was their custom to depart, and to meet again at a common but innocent meal, which they had left off upon that edict which I published at your command, and wherein I had forbidden any such conventiclers. These examinations made me think it necessary to inquire by torments what the truth was; which I did of the two servant maids, who were called Deaconesses; but still I discovered no more than that they were addicted to a bad and to an extravagant superstition.

Hereupon, I have put off any further examinations, and have recourse to you, for the affair seems to be well worth consultation, especially on account of the number of those that are in danger; for there are many of every age, of every rank, and of both sexes, who are now and hereafter likely to be called to account, and to be in danger; for this superstition is spread like a contagion, not only into cities and towns, but into country villages also, which yet there is reason to hope may be stopped and corrected. To be sure, the temples, which were almost forsaken, begin already to be frequented; and the holy solemnities, which were long intermitted, begin to be revived. The sacrifices begin to sell well everywhere, of which very few purchasers had of late appeared; whereby it is easy to suppose how great a multitude of men may be amended, if place for repentance be admitted.[6]

It is most interesting to go back in time and actually feel the events taking place at the time of Christian persecution. Here we see the result of an impassioned letter to the emperor of Rome that describes the judgmental process and capital punishment end to those proclaiming Christianity. While we are aware that there are many Christians who chose death over cursing Jesus, the letter also describes in vivid detail those who *did* recant their faith to save their lives—in other words those who "sold out" Christ to worship Emperor Trajan. One wonders how committed they were to Jesus in the first place.

The letter also points out the strength of the belief in the resurrection (the "bad" superstition). According to the letter, the believers in Jesus spanned a broad group of people—young, old; male, female; and of every social class. And it references how quickly it was spreading throughout the region.

References to Jesus by the Historian Suetonius

Caius Suetonius Tranquillus was the private secretary of Emperor Hadrian. We know that Hadrian was very concerned about the spread of Christianity. He was so concerned that he covered up the holy sites of the crucifixion and the resurrection with pagan statues in an attempt to "help" Christians forget them. Obviously there was discussion of Jesus and the Christians between Hadrian and Suetonius.

Suetonius was an ancient historian who lived from about A.D. 69 to 140. Apart from his relationship to Hadrian, little is known about his life. He did write many ancient historical works that we still have today, including *De vita Caesarum* (about the lives of the Caesars, translated into English in 1957 by Robert Graves as *The Twelve Caesars*) and the much larger collection of biographies *De viris illustribus* (concerning illustrious men).

The actual words Suetonius wrote about Jesus Christ and the Christians are:

> Because the Jews at Rome caused constant disturbances at the instigation of Chrestus (Christ), he (Claudius) expelled them from the city of (Rome).
>
> —Suetonius' *Life of the Emperor Claudius*,
> chapter 25 (excerpt)[7]

During his reign many abuses were severely punished and put down, and no fewer new laws were
made; a limit was set to expenditures, the public ban-
quets were confined to a distribution of food, the sale of
any kind of cooked viands in the taverns was forbidden, with the exception of pulse and vegetables,
whereas before every sort of dainty was exposed for
sale. Punishment was inflicted on the Christians, a class
of men given to a new and mischievous superstition.
He put an end to the diversions of the chariot drivers,
who from immunity of long standing claimed the right
of ranging at large and amusing themselves by cheating
and robbing the people. The pantomimic actors and
their partisans were banished from the city.

—Suetonius' *Life of the Emperor Nero,*
chapter 16 (excerpt)[8]

Suetonius reaffirms the historicity of the belief in the resurrection, like other ancient historians that were nonbelievers, calling it
a "superstition."

Reference to Jesus by the Historian Phlegon

The early church father Origen was seeking ancient writings by
non-Christian historians about the events of the crucifixion and resurrection. He was told of writing by Phlegon, who wrote about the
events of the earthquakes and darkened sky at the time of the crucifixion.

Phlegon blamed the darkness at the time of the crucifixion on
a solar eclipse, which Origen refutes. Ironically, we know that scientifically a solar eclipse would be impossible at Passover (the
time of Jesus' crucifixion) because Passover is timed when there is
a full moon. It would be scientifically impossible for a solar

eclipse to occur then because the moon would be on the wrong side of the earth.

Origen (A.D. 184–254) references two works by Phlegon: 1) Chronicles and 2) Olympiads. Unfortunately both originals by Phlegon have been lost. Only the references to them by Origen remain. The citations in which Origen addresses the mistaken solar eclipse at the time of the crucifixion, are:

> And with regard to the eclipse in the time of Tiberius Caesar, in whose reign Jesus appears to have been crucified, and the great earthquakes which then took place...[9]
>
> —Origen against Celsus

> Phlegon mentioned the eclipse which took place during the crucifixion of the Lord Jesus and no other (eclipse); it is clear that he did not know from his sources about any (similar) eclipse in previous times and this is shown by the historical account of Tiberius Caesar.[10]
>
> —Origen and Philopon, *De. Opif. Mund.* II21

Phlegon also referred to Jesus' prophecy and indicated that the prophecies came true.

> Now Phlegon, in the thirteenth or fourteenth book, I think of his Chronicles, not only ascribed to Jesus a knowledge of future events...but also testified that the result corresponded to his predictions.[11]
>
> —Origen against Celsus

Phlegon's extrabiblical writing provides support of the events as described in the Bible. Although he was not a Christian, he did not deny the events, and he even supported the prophetic accuracy of Jesus.

References of Jesus by Satirist Lucian of Samosata

The satirist Lucian had a passion for history and the truth. This passion is recorded in some of his writings:

> History... abhors the intrusion of any least scruple of falsehood; it is like the windpipe, which the doctors tell us will not tolerate a morsel of stray food.

> The historian's one task is to tell the thing as it happened.

> [The historian] must sacrifice to no God but Truth; he must neglect all else; his sole rule and unerring guide is this—to think not of those who are listening to him now, but of the yet unborn who shall seek his converse.

This conviction to history and the truth is important when we consider his writings regarding Jesus (especially considering that he is a satirist who would tend to poke fun at things).

Lucian was born in Samosata, and lived from about A.D. 125 to 180. He was the son of a sculptor, but quickly decided not to pursue the same career and chose instead to pursue a career of rhetoric and later public speaking in such locations as Ionia, Greece, Italy, and even Gaul. His speaking was self-proclaimed to simply amuse, not to establish any moral truths or philosophize. He was, however, a lover of historical accuracy and truth as the previous quotes indicate.

Lucian frequently poked fun at the Christians whom he regarded as simple and gullible. He wrote:

> The Christians... worship a man to this day—the distinguished personage who introduced their novel rites, and was crucified on that account....[It] was impressed on them by their original lawgiver that they are all brothers, from the moment that they are converted, and

deny the gods of Greece, and worship the crucified sage, and live after his laws.[12]

Although making fun of Christians in this statement, several points are worth noting: 1) that Jesus is referred to as a man, 2) that his "novel rites" are noted, 3) that he was crucified, 4) that his followers thought highly of him, 5) that the followers were *converted from the gods* of Greece to 6) *worship the "sage."*

References to Jesus from Emperor Hadrian

Hadrian, the emperor of Rome from A.D. 117–138, had a significant impact on the Jewish and Christian world. In an attempt to rid Christians of any memories of holy sites of Jesus, he built a pagan temple over the site of the crucifixion and placed statues of Venus on the place of the crucifixion and Jupiter on the place of the resurrection. Far from causing Christians to forget these sites, they only served as markers, allowing them to be revered as holy sites later on.

Hadrian's hated actions—forbidding several Jewish customs, building pagan monuments, and taxing the Jews and Christians in the name of pagan gods—led to a Jewish revolt, which was put down in 132. Once the revolt was over, Jews were not permitted back into the city of Jerusalem—and most Christians in the region were Jews.

Hadrian seemed to be more tolerant of Christians than other Roman leaders during persecution, and in a letter written to the proconsul of Asia in 124 he warns against false accusation:

> I do not wish, therefore, that the matter should be passed by without examination, so that these men may neither be harassed, nor opportunity of malicious proceedings be offered to informers. If, therefore, the provincials can clearly evince their charges against the

Christians, so as to answer before the tribunal, let them pursue this course only, but not by mere petitions, and mere outcries against the Christians. For it is far more proper, if anyone would bring an accusation, that you should examine it.

Hadrian further explained that if Christians were found guilty they should be judged "according to the heinousness of the crime." If the accusers were only slandering the believers, then those who inaccurately made the charges were to be punished.[13]

However, not to be misled, during organized massacres, such niceties didn't apply. Also, like at other times, Christians were required to worship Roman gods (especially Jupiter) and refusal to renounce their faith and bow down to Roman gods resulted in execution.

Hadrian's policies (even to the extent of attempting to mask the holy sites) and writings provide non-Christian evidence contemporary with some eyewitnesses to Jesus of the rapid spread of Christianity and of the strong belief in the resurrection.

CONCLUSION

Considering that there are not many works of any kind that still exist from the first and second centuries, there is considerable non-Christian evidence of Jesus Christ. This evidence is 100 percent in agreement with the account of the life and death of Jesus in the Bible. Although ancient non-believers obviously doubt the resurrection, they acknowledge its widespread acceptance (calling it a superstition). In addition, non-Christian writings talk about Jesus' miracles, his crucifixion, and many other details about him and his followers. Since even such enemies of Jesus acknowledge him and his works, there is little doubt regarding his historical existence.

Archaeological
Sites of Jesus

The women excitedly talked about the traders who had come to Nazareth bringing bright new fabrics and special perfumes. Although none of the women could afford any of the special items, it didn't stop them from admiring the traders' wares and spending countless hours dreaming about them. The town well, where all the women in the area went for water in the morning, was the best place for news, swapping stories, and just plain gossip.

Mary, the daughter of Heli, was like so many of the young ladies in the village—a peasant girl who helped with daily tasks of getting water, cooking, cleaning, and making clothing. She was around 16 years old, and was betrothed to Joseph, a young local man who was learning how to be a carpenter. Today seemed like any other day except for the excitement the women shared discussing the traders in town.

After the morning at the well, Mary ambled home and went into a small room in her house where she commonly went to spin yarn. Suddenly and without warning an incredible apparition of an angel appeared.

"Greetings, you who are highly favored! The Lord is with you."

Mary was greatly troubled at his words and wondered what kind of greeting this might be. But the angel said to her, "Do not be afraid, Mary, you have found favor with God. You will be with child and give birth to a son, and you are to give him the name Jesus. He will be great and will be called the Son of the Most High. The Lord God will give him the throne of his father David, and he will reign over the house of Jacob forever; his kingdom will never end."

"How will this be," Mary asked the angel, "since I am a virgin?"

The angel answered, "The Holy Spirit will come upon you, and the power of the Most High will overshadow you. So the holy one to be born will be called the Son of God. Even Elizabeth your relative is going to have a child in her old age, and she who was said to be barren is in her sixth month. For nothing is impossible with God."

"I am the Lord's servant," Mary answered. "May it be to me as you have said." Then the angel left her (Luke 1:28-38).

Site of the Annunciation of Jesus to Mary

The site of the annunciation of the coming of Jesus by the angel Gabriel (as described in the Bible) has been venerated since the fourth century. Certainly such a dramatic event as the annunciation of a miracle birth by an angel would certainly not be forgotten by Mary, and presumably she related the story to her family many times as well. Hence, Mary's family and friends would have recalled the location. Historical records by non-Christian sources indicate that ancestors of Jesus remained in Nazareth at least until the third century and perhaps much longer. Therefore, it would not be surprising for word of mouth to maintain the correct identification of the site until the first church was built upon it in the third century. Remains of the original church have been found and dated by its architecture and early period graffiti.

Underneath the current church are two grottos. The larger one is believed to be the actual place where Mary saw the angel (church tradition says while "spinning scarlet thread"). It may have been a dwelling or possibly an underground storeroom common to the period. The grottos also contain elaborate floor mosaics. One mosaic contains a pattern of crosses that abruptly ceases, indicating it was probably under construction in A.D. 427 when Emperor Theodosius II issued an edict forbidding the decoration of floors with the images of crosses. The second, smaller grotto has been identified as honoring the martyr Conon, a relative of Jesus, who was put to death around the year 250 in Asia Minor.[1]

ANOTHER OBVIOUSLY AUTHENTIC ARCHAEOLOGICAL SITE related to the life of Jesus is the well at Nazareth. It is the only water source in the tiny village. So without question Mary and Jesus would have retrieved water from the well. Even today, people can visit the well, and drink from the same source that supplied the family of Jesus.

Some people believe there were actually two sites of annunciation by the angel Gabriel—the first at the well (Luke 1:26-28 in which Mary is simply told that the "Lord is with you") and the second at the site venerated for the annunciation.

Biblical archaeology does not prove most events (it doesn't specifically prove the annunciation took place). What archaeology can do is verify either that 1) people believed certain events took place—shown by veneration of such sites, or 2) that conditions were met that support the account of events as written in the Bible.

In the case of the annunciation, we know that the early Christians did believe that the events took place at the site(s) and that there were no conditions that would have precluded the biblical story.

The Site of Jesus' Birth

Archaeologists have identified the probable site of Jesus' birth in the city of Bethlehem, approximately five miles outside of Jerusalem. Unlike the wooden stables so often represented in commercial Christmas displays, the actual stable was almost certainly a cave, which was quite typical in the first century.

Several things would lead us to the conclusion that the site is authentic. First, the events surrounding the birth of Jesus were dramatic and memorable. It was no ordinary birth: 1) Zechariah (John the Baptist's father) lost his speech and miraculously regained it, then proclaimed his son as the forerunner to Jesus. 2) Elizabeth (John the Baptist's mother) recognized Mary as the mother of the Messiah (Luke 1:41-45). 3) Angels appeared to shepherds who ran around Bethlehem announcing the birth of Jesus. 4) Simeon recognized Jesus as the Messiah (Luke 2:25-35). 5) Anna recognized Jesus as the Messiah (Luke 2:36-38). 6) Powerful Magi rode into town (Matthew 2:1-12). 7) Herod ordered the killing of male children two years old and under (Matthew 2:16). The birth of Jesus was anything but ordinary; it was highly memorable.

Today, even with the most ordinary of births, family and friends recall where the birth took place. Why would anyone think things were different at the time of Jesus? Add to that the many other people who were undoubtedly aware of the birth (due to the shepherds, the Magi, the killings caused by Herod), and we have a considerable number of people who would be aware of the site. Later, as the mission of Jesus was revealed through his death and resurrection, early Christian leaders marked and venerated the many significant sites of Jesus' ministry. It was not unlike great leaders today, who often have early childhood homes marked as historical sites.

So great was Rome's concern about the veneration of Jesus, that the Romans often constructed statues of pagan gods over Christian sites, as Emperor Hadrian did at the sites of the crucifixion and resurrection. However this only served to "mark" the sites until persecution was stopped by Constantine. In the case of the site of the nativity, Hadrian planted a grove of trees there honoring the pagan god Adonis. When Constantine ended persecution, he sent his mother, Helena, to the holy lands to mark several sites of Jesus. The ancient historian Eusebius wrote that the emperor and his mother constructed a church over the cave of the birth of Jesus and lavishly adorned it.[2] Since then several churches have been constructed on the site over earlier ones that had been repeatedly torn down as foreign rulers occupied the land.

It is by excavating the historical churches, built as monuments on this site over the centuries, that we can have confidence in its authenticity. It is fully consistent with the biblical record.

The Cave of Jesus' End-Time Revelation

Jesus gave his famous Olivet Discourse (Matthew 24–25) on the Mount of Olives toward the end of his ministry. In this well-known revelation to his disciples, Jesus reviews in some detail the events leading up to and occurring at the end of time. Certainly this would have been a memorable event for the disciples, and presumably one they told others about later. Therefore, it would be natural for early Christians to remember and later venerate the site where this occurred. And, in fact, they did.

Eusebius, writing in the early 300s, told of a church that was erected to honor the cave where Jesus gave the end-time revelations. Excavation has located this church, which was built by Helena Augusta, Constantine's mother. Other corroboration of the erection of a church by Helena within 300 years of Jesus' resurrection includes: 1) The Bordeaux Pilgrim, who upon seeing the church in 333 said it was located at the place "where before the Passion, the Lord taught the disciples," 2) Aetheria (381–384) indicated that "the cave in which the Lord used to teach is there," and 3) Nicephorus (829) tells of climbing marble stairs built to lead up to the church built by Helena.[3]

The Site of the Last Supper

The Last Supper is believed to have taken place in the house belonging to John Mark's mother. Other events said to have taken place there include 1) Jesus' washing of the disciples' feet; 2) the meeting of the disciples after the resurrection (Luke 24:33-49); 3) the receiving of the Holy Spirit by the disciples at Pentecost (Acts 2:1-4); and 4) the death of Jesus' mother, Mary. Early Christians identified the site and many writers later confirmed it, including Origen (in 250), Eusebius (in 300), Aetheria (in 381), Jerome (in 400), and Theodosius (in 530).

A "great church" was built on the site—located on Mount Zion only 200 "paces" from Golgotha (the site of the crucifixion of Jesus). The church was destroyed by the Persians in 614 and later rebuilt.

Excavations in and around the church have located part of a first-century "synagogue" that seems to be similar to the "house-synagogue" created in the house of Peter after the resurrection (see pages 140–41). It may have been built in the house of John Mark's mother. Interestingly, a niche that was used to hold Holy Scripture was oriented toward Golgotha instead of in the customary direction toward the Temple. This probably reflected a change in worship based on Jesus' once-and-for-all sacrifice.

The Site of the Crucifixion of Jesus

All four gospels mention Golgotha (translated as "place of the skull") as the site of the crucifixion of Jesus.

> They came to a place called Golgotha (which means The Place of the Skull) (Matthew 27:33).

> They brought Jesus to the place called Golgotha (which means The Place of the Skull) (Mark 15:22).

> When they came to the place called the Skull, there they crucified him, along with the criminals—one on his right, the other on his left (Luke 23:33).

> Carrying his own cross, he went out to the place of the Skull (which in Aramaic is called Golgotha) (John 19:17).

The site of Golgotha is certainly one of the two most important historical sites of Christianity (the other being the site of the resurrection). Given that, it would be expected that early Christians would have immediately venerated the site. This is borne out by historical records. Eusebius, the noted church historian (263–339) spoke in a church constructed by Helena, Constantine's mother, to mark the sites of Jesus' death and resurrection soon after the end of persecution in 313. He remarked that all that was required was to remove a small temple of Venus constructed by Hadrian in 135, over the site of the crucifixion. Hadrian had hoped to draw Christian attention away from the holy site, but his efforts were in vain.

Further confirming the likelihood of the accurate identification of the site of the crucifixion by Helena is that she marked it inside the city walls, when customarily a crucifixion site would be outside the city. Why did she do so? King Agrippa I built a new wall on the north side of Jerusalem within 15 years of the death of Jesus. Unless there had been a compelling reason to do so, Helena would not have been expected to find the true site inside the city. However something as holy as the site of Jesus' death would certainly be remembered for generations to come. And the placement of the Temple of Venus at the site by Hadrian would have made finding the location very easy.

The Site of the Resurrection of Jesus

The tomb of the resurrection of Jesus (along with the site of the crucifixion) is undoubtedly the single most venerated site in all Christianity. Certainly the early Christians would have done everything to mark the location since it represented the foundation of Christianity itself. The importance is borne out by the historical record. The ancient historian Jerome, writing to Paulinus in A.D. 395 indicated that Hadrian intended to wipe out any memory of the key sites of Jesus by 1) removing the Jews (many of whom were Christians) from Jerusalem, 2) erecting a temple to Venus at the site of Golgotha, and 3) erecting a statue to Jupiter at the site of the tomb of Jesus. Eusebius also confirmed the unintentional marking of the holy sites by the pagan structures.[4]

Today the Church of the Holy Sepulcher encloses both of these probable sites—one at each end. The original church was constructed by Helena, mother of Constantine, but like many other churches established on holy sites, it was repeatedly razed and rebuilt over the centuries.

In A.D. 326, Emperor Constantine's mother, Helena—a devout Christian—was disturbed when the Bishop of Aelia Capitolina described the sad neglect of holy sites of Jesus during the period of the persecution. This prompted Constantine to approve his mother's request to fund her visit to establish and honor key sites of Jesus.

The sites of the crucifixion and resurrection were two of the holiest sites of Jesus that were relatively easy to discover. History records that Helena quickly identified the sites due to the pagan temples and statuary that had been erected there by Emperor Hadrian.

Once Helena had the existing Roman structures destroyed, they identified the rock that was named Golgotha, and also found a network of tombs—one of which they identified as that owned by Joseph of Arimathea. Once the sloping bedrock was cut away around the tomb it left a shell at the site of the present-day edicule.[5]

Site of the Ascension of Jesus

Jesus' last act on earth was his ascension into heaven (Luke 24:50-53; Acts 1:9). The place of this event was noted by early Christian writers (for example, Aetheria in A.D. 381), but no mention of a church was made. A Church of the Ascension was built by the pilgrim Egeria in the fourth century, and it was verified as existing by the year 404, when it was described by Jerome. Destroyed by the Persians in 614, it was rebuilt by the year 670, when Arculf speaks of the "last footprints" of the Lord being visible by the light of an "eternally" burning lamp. In 1187 the church was taken over by the Muslims and turned into a mosque, which it remains today.

A "step" in the rock where Jesus is said to have ascended has been preserved inside the church/mosque.[6]

CONCLUSION

The discovery of many of the probable archaeological sites of the ministry, death, and resurrection of Jesus provides insights regarding the strength of the belief of the people at the time and that the events the sites represent are historically valid.

Other Archaeological Support for Jesus

John, Amos, and Stephan ran around the back of the house of Peter the fisherman and hid behind the bushes to see what the men would do next. Excitement filled the air! Jesus, the famous miracle worker, was inside. The entire town of Capernaum was abuzz. Crowds packed the front door. Nobody else could hope to get a chance to even see Jesus. But the boys could hear Jesus speaking to the people within. He spoke of the kingdom of heaven, of the grace of God, and of eternal life.

But what caught the boys' attention were four men who had just arrived carrying poor Barnabas on a mat. Everyone in the city knew Barnabas had been paralyzed since birth and had no hope of ever living a normal life. The men would not be able to break through the crowds in the front of the house, and the boys figured that something was up. As they had suspected, the men had gone around to the back and were climbing the stairs to the roof.

Since they could not get him to Jesus because of the crowd, they made an opening in the roof above Jesus and, after digging through it, lowered the mat the paralyzed man was lying on. When Jesus saw their faith, he said to the paralytic, "Son, your sins are forgiven."

Now some teachers of the law were sitting there, thinking to themselves, "Why does this fellow talk like that? He's blaspheming! Who can forgive sins but God alone?"

Immediately Jesus knew in his spirit that this was what they were thinking in their hearts, and he said to them, "Why are you thinking these things? Which is easier: to say to the paralytic, 'Your sins are forgiven,' or to say, 'Get up, take your mat and walk'? But that you may know that the Son of Man has authority on earth to forgive sins...." He said to the paralytic, "I tell you, get up, take your mat and go home." He got up, took his mat and walked out in full view of them all. This amazed everyone and they praised God, saying, "We have never seen anything like this!" (Mark 2:4-12).

The House of the Apostle Peter

Ancient pilgrims had written about an octagonal church converted from the "house of the chief of the apostles." Although lands containing an octagonal structure had been held in custody in Capernaum since 1906, it wasn't until 1968 that the Franciscan archaeologist Virgilio Corbo began careful excavation. What he eventually found was a fifth-century church built atop a "house church" dating to the fourth century, which lay on top of a simple "courtyard house" from the first century.

One room of the house contained many invocations in Aramaic, Greek, Hebrew, Latin, and Syriac scratched into the walls. Several clues indicated that the room carried special significance to first-century Christians and was revered by later generations. Walls of the room had been replastered at least twice, and normal domestic pottery had ceased to be used in the room since the mid-first century, indicating the room had some other special significance (such as a "house church").

The construction of the house was typical of the city, and it had walls that would not support a second story or a masonry roof. The walls would, however, support the kind of thatched roof indicated in the house of Peter in the Bible (Mark 2:4). The continuous reverence attached to the house with churches built on top of churches, along with sustained identification of the site as the house of Peter through the centuries lends credence to the accuracy of the claim.

The Tomb of Lazarus

The small town of Bethany has revealed an abundance of archaeological discoveries from the time of Jesus. One area of Bethany is honeycombed with tombs, one of which has been identified as the tomb of Lazarus.

Several details lead many archaeologists to believe the tomb is authentic. First, the identification of the village and the site is generally accepted. Second, the artifacts found are consistent with the period. Third, there is substantial evidence that contemporaries to the event believed it to be the actual site of the tomb. The evidence includes early graffiti written by Christians that refer to Lazarus being raised from the dead there and request similar mercy for the writers themselves.

Like many other events surrounding the life of Jesus, the resurrection of Lazarus was unforgettable. In fact, it was one of the most unforgettable events of all, causing religious leaders to hasten their attempt to execute Jesus. Given that it was highly memorable, it's not surprising that the site was marked and venerated from the earliest days—as the graffiti at the site indicates. This discovery is an exciting addition to the archaeological reasons supporting the belief in the gospel account of Jesus.

The First-Century Fishing Boat

The droughts in Israel in the 1980s caused great hardship to the people and caused the water level of the Sea of Galilee to drop significantly. However, the receding water exposed a well-preserved first-century fishing boat stuck in the mud not far from the new shoreline. Under the direction of the Israel Antiquities Authority, a race against time was initiated to carefully extract the boat from the mud without damage before the waters returned. A complex system of dikes and hydraulics was set up to slowly raise the boat from the sea. Eventually it was placed in a climate-controlled environment to protect it from aging. The fishing boat was of the type described in the Gospels:

> One day Jesus said to his disciples, "Let's go over to the other side of the lake." So they got into a boat and set out. As they sailed, he fell asleep. A squall came down on the lake, so that the boat was being swamped, and they were in great danger.
>
> The disciples went and woke him, saying, "Master, Master, we're going to drown!"
>
> He got up and rebuked the wind and the raging waters; the storm subsided, and all was calm. "Where is your faith?" he asked his disciples.
>
> In fear and amazement they asked one another, "Who is this? He commands even the winds and the water, and they obey him" (Luke 8:22-25).

Pots and lamps found inside the boat dated it to the first century. Carbon 14 testing further confirmed the dating. The design of the boat was typical of fishing boats used during that period on the Sea of Galilee. In the back of the boat was a raised section where Jesus could have been sleeping, as indicated in the gospel accounts. The boat could accommodate 15 people including crew. The descriptions of the fishing boats mentioned in the Bible during the time of Jesus' ministry in Galilee are confirmed through archaeology.

The Inscription of Pontius Pilate

In 1961 archaeologists were clearing sand from the ruins of a theater in the Roman capital city of Caesarea Maritima when they came across a stone, turned upside down, bearing the name Pontius Pilate—Roman prefect of Judea (see Luke 3:1). The plaque boasted that Pilate was dedicating a newly built Tiberium to Emperor Tiberius.[1]

Archaeologists indicate the stone was certainly not in its original position, but had been reused in a theater construction in the fourth century. It was an important find for several reasons. First, it established the existence of Pontius Pilate through archaeology (in addition to the manuscripts that have indicated his existence). Second, it settled a dispute that Pilate was, in fact, a prefect (governor) instead of the inferior procurator, as some people had thought. Third, it corroborated a timing link to Tiberius Caesar. And finally, it demonstrated Pilate's desire to appeal to the graces of Tiberius in his affairs.

Proof of Crucifixion

In June 1968, the Israel Antiquities Authority excavated some burial caves northeast of Jerusalem. Inside one family tomb, five ossuaries were discovered. One contained the skeletons of two men and a young child. One of the men had a heel bone with a 4½-inch spike that had been nailed through a small board to prevent the heel from tearing through the nail head. The man was five foot five inches tall and was in his mid-twenties. His hands had been tied to the cross, not nailed like many others. The ossuary bore his name, Yehochanan.

Death by crucifixion was, perhaps, the most horrible, painful death ever conceived by man. Spikes were nailed between the bones in the wrist, not in the hands as commonly thought (because the weight of the hanging body would cause the spikes to tear the flesh from the hands, thus freeing the victim). Spikes were also nailed through the feet, or the heels of the victim (various positions were used). Death occurred, not through loss of blood, but by suffocation. In order to breath, the victim had to push up on the nails in the feet, releasing pressure on the diaphragm. This caused great pain in the nailed feet. Fatigue would then cause the victim to sag back down. However the nails in the wrists tore into a concentrated section of nerves. As the victim sagged down, he could not breathe, until finally again, he pushed up from his feet. Up. Down. Up. Down. Eventually, fatigue would take its toll and the victim would die. Occasionally, people being crucified would survive for several days. And often the Roman executors would break the legs of the victims to hasten death (they could not push up to breathe with broken legs).

The heel of the skeleton provides evidence of crucifixion methods described in the Bible, corroborating first-century accounts of Roman crucifixion in Jerusalem.

The Ossuary of James

Probably one of the greatest archaeological discoveries ever is the finding of an ossuary of James, the first leader of the church in Jerusalem and the brother of Jesus. Some say it rivals the finding of the Dead Sea Scrolls in importance (I disagree since the Dead Sea Scrolls validate the all-important prophecies of Jesus).

The ossuary of James, recently "rediscovered" in Israel, is similar to the hundreds of ossuaries that have been found. Ossuaries are limestone boxes measuring approximately 1.25 feet by 2.5 feet that were in common usage from about 100 B.C. until A.D. 70. The purpose of ossuaries was to free up expensive and rare tomb space by moving bones to another location one year after burial of the deceased (after the flesh had decomposed).

The "James ossuary" is unique because an Aramaic inscription reads, "James, son of Joseph, brother of Jesus." Although skeptics may question whether, in fact, the Joseph and Jesus are those mentioned in the New Testament, it is highly unlikely that they are not. No one questions that the names James, Joseph, and Jesus were in common usage at the time of the first century. However, an ossuary with all three names would be statistically rare. Such inscriptions are also rare—especially when a brother is mentioned. This indicates that the brother was probably very important or well known. If this ossuary held the bones of James the brother of Jesus of Nazareth, it's an amazing discovery and further proof of the existence of Jesus!

Despite a long history of archaeological forgeries in Israel, this ossuary is probably genuine:

- The grammar and script of the writing fits normal usage of the writing leading up to the destruction of Jerusalem in A.D. 70.

- Laboratory tests reveal no traces of modern elements on the ossuary.

- Analysis under the electron microscope shows no indication of modern tooling used in formation of any letters or decoration.

- There is evidence of "patina," even in the recesses of the inscription. (Patina is a microscopic film that can only be developed over many centuries of the box being stored in a cave or a tomb.)

- Some experts from the Israeli government confirmed that "there is no evidence of modern tinkering" or forgery.

If genuine, the ossuary of James provides archaeological proof of the existence of Jesus and James and their relationship.

The Ossuary of Caiaphus

In November 1990 construction workers in a section south of Jerusalem's Old City broke through a burial cave that had been sealed since Rome had destroyed the city in A.D. 70. Inside they found an ornately decorated ossuary—a box that contained the bones of a deceased person. But this ossuary was no ordinary find. Etched on the side, in ancient Aramaic, was the name "Caiaphas." That inscription, along with other inscriptions of family members in the tomb, made it clear that this was the actual ossuary of Caiaphas, the high priest who first sought to kill Jesus: "Then the chief priests and the elders of the people assembled in the palace of the high priest, whose name was Caiaphas, and they plotted to arrest Jesus in some sly way and kill him" (Matthew 26:3-4).

Caiaphas was not only instrumental in leading the plot to kill Jesus, he actually presided over the first trial (by the religious leaders) in which Jesus was convicted—by his confession—of the capital offense of blasphemy!

> The high priest said to him, "I charge you under oath by the living God: Tell us if you are the Christ, the Son of God."
>
> "Yes, it is as you say," Jesus replied. "But I say to all of you: In the future you will see the Son of Man sitting at the right hand of the Mighty One and coming on the clouds of heaven."

Then the high priest tore his clothes and said, "He has spoken blasphemy! Why do we need any more witnesses? Look, now you have heard the blasphemy. What do you think?"

"He is worthy of death," they answered (Matthew 26:63-66).

The ossuary of Caiaphas doesn't prove the resurrection of Jesus; however, it is one further piece of evidence of the people involved in Jesus' trial, death, and resurrection.

Christian Ossuaries in Jerusalem

The discovery of two ossuaries outside of Jerusalem in 1945 by Eleazar L. Sukenik provided interesting insights about first-century Christians. The ossuaries were marked with graffiti and four crosses. The words "Iesous iou" were found, which essentially meant "Jesus help." Also found were the words "Iesous aloth," which essentially meant "Jesus let him arise."[2]

Experts date the ossuaries to about A.D. 50, which would have been within twenty years of Jesus' death and resurrection. Certainly there would have been many eyewitnesses in Jerusalem at that time. Possibly, even those writing on the ossuaries were eyewitnesses.

The writing and crosses imply:

1. confirmation of the crucifixion of Jesus

2. confirmation of belief that Jesus had some power to provide resurrection

3. confirmation that Jesus could perform miracles

The two ossuaries indicate strong belief of at least some people in Jerusalem—about the time of Jesus—that Jesus had, in fact, been crucified and had the power to provide resurrection.

CONCLUSION

The wealth of miscellaneous archaeological evidence—from the house of Peter to the tomb of Lazarus, from the evidence of cultural claims in the Bible to ossuaries of actual people named in the Bible—points to the accuracy of the biblical account regarding Jesus.

Great Archaeologists Convert to Christianity

The tension in the air was enormous; one could cut it with a knife. The crowd of the most highly esteemed archaeologists had been invited for announcement of the final conclusion about a scroll of Isaiah that was discovered by accident among caves located along the Dead Sea. The great archaeologist William F. Albright would be making the announcement himself. Everyone was murmuring with nervous excitement.

Then Albright appeared and the room suddenly became deathly silent.

"Ladies and gentlemen," Albright began, "a most incredible find amongst the Qumran caves has been discovered. It's a scroll of Isaiah, that has been found in its entirety and was written by the Essene sect of the Jews some 200 years B.C. This predates the earliest known copy of Isaiah by hundreds of years.

"I repeat that in my opinion [Mr. Trevor has] made the

greatest manuscript discovery of modern times—certainly the greatest biblical manuscript find....What an incredible find!"[1]

ONCE A DIRECTOR OF THE SCHOOL OF ORIENTAL RESEARCH at Johns Hopkins University, William Albright (1891–1971) wrote more than 800 books and articles, mostly on the validity of biblical manuscripts. He is best known for his work in confirming the authenticity of the Old Testament, which contains well over 100 prophecies of Jesus Christ.

Albright is also well known for his authentication of the Dead Sea Scrolls. Since these scrolls ensure that Old Testament prophecies were written *before* the time of Jesus, we can be certain that the prophecies were not contrived after the fact. The scroll of Isaiah, which was found in "near-perfect" condition, contains 23 prophecies in Isaiah chapter 53 alone—a nearly perfect description of Jesus, the Messiah to come. By confirming that the Old Testament prophecies were written before the time of Christ, especially considering the number of specific prophecies, one can calculate statistically that they would be impossible to all come true in one human being without divine intervention (see chapters 14–16).

Albright also researched and confirmed the dating of the writings of the New Testament. His conclusion is that there is "no longer any solid basis for dating any book of the New Testament after about A.D. 80."[2]

Early in his professional life, William F. Albright had some doubts about the validity of biblical claims about Jesus. These, however, were answered conclusively in favor of the authenticity of the Bible as he conducted his research.

Sir William Ramsay

Sir William Ramsay was, arguably, the greatest archaeologist of his day. He had rejected much of the written New Testament account and was determined to prove it false based on other writings of the day that contradicted the Bible. Ramsay's archaeological digs were long and arduous. Imagine this scenario based on the facts:

> Dirt caked on their shoes broke off in chunks and tumbled to the ground. Dust, rubbing like ever present sandpaper, filled every cavity in their clothing. The sun was setting. Only the distinctive sound of metal cutting through dirt and rock broke the silence. It had been a long hard day, and the team of archaeologists was dead tired.
>
> "I've got something here!" yelled George as his shovel broke away a large glob of earth exposing the top of what appeared to be an ancient stone etched with writing. "Come and take a look."
>
> The great archeologist, Sir William Ramsay hurried over to see what was discovered as George and the others meticulously uncovered their find. After what seemed like hours, it was in full view for inspection by Ramsay and his team. It was an ancient monument that bore writing that included an important reference to cities in the area of Asia Minor—precisely what Ramsay was looking for.
>
> "Ahhh," Ramsay exclaimed. "Notice here the reference to Iconium. It clearly indicates that the city is a Phrygian city, or a city in Lycaonia—along with Derby and Lystra—just as Luke proclaimed in the Bible. How interesting! This refutes what my archaeologist collegues have long thought, based on the Roman writing of Cicero. Again, the Bible is right (Acts 13; 14:6).

Sir William Ramsay made this discovery in 1910, as one of many such discoveries in his quest to prove Luke wrong. He hoped to confirm what many archaeologists had once thought—

that the Bible was full of errors. Ramsay believed that the books of Luke and Acts were actually written in about A.D. 150, and therefore did not bear the authenticity that a first-century document would. His archaeological journeys took him to 32 countries, 44 cities, and 9 islands.[3] Throughout some 15 years of intensive study, he concluded that "Luke is a historian of the first rank—this author should be placed along with the very greatest of historians."

Many archaeologists in the nineteenth century thought the Bible was full of errors, and Ramsay thought his search would discredit the Bible. However, in every case the Bible was confirmed. Some popular misconceptions that Ramsay helped correct are:

Critics Thought...	Ramsay Discovered...
there was no Roman census (as indicated in Luke 2:1).	there was a Roman census every 14 years beginning with Emperor Augustus.
Quirinius was not governor of Syria at the time of Jesus' birth (as indicated in Luke 2:2).	that Quirinius was governor of Syria in about 7 B.C.
people did not have to return to their ancestral home (as indicated in Luke 2:3).	that people did have to return to their home city—verified by an ancient Egyptian papyrus giving directions for conducting a census.
the existence of the treasurer of the city of Corinth, Erastus (Romans 16:23), was incorrect.	a city pavement in Corinth bearing the inscription "Erastus, curator of public buildings, laid this pavement at his own expense."
Luke's reference to Gallio as proconsul of Achaia was wrong (Acts 18:12).	the Delphi inscription that reads, "As Lucius Junius Gallio, my friend and proconsul of Achaia."

Time and time again Ramsay's search to find evidence that Luke's writing was in error turned up evidence that it was, in fact, accurate. As a result, Sir William Ramsay eventually converted to Christianity and proclaimed Luke as "one of the greatest historians" of all time.

CONCLUSION

The fact that two of the greatest archaeologists of all time made a systematic study to refute the Bible—and ended up finding evidence in support of it strongly supports biblical claims. The fact that both of these archaeological skeptics ended up following the Christianity they once doubted is powerful testimony to their individual integrity and beliefs.

Miraculous Prophecy Forecasts Jesus' Life and Ministry

B ut Mary is pregnant and due any time now!" Joseph pleaded with the innkeeper, hoping that he could find some way to accommodate them in the city of Bethlehem.

"Sorry," the innkeeper said. "What am I supposed to do, ask someone to leave who has already paid for a room?"

"What can we do?" Joseph said. "Surely there is someplace to go other than the streets. Please! My dear wife is about to have a baby!"

"I'll tell you what," the innkeeper responded, "I've got a stable out back that you are welcome to use. It's no inn, but it'll keep you dry. It's better than nothing."

"Mary, what do you think?" Joseph asked. "It's either this or trek back to Jerusalem—and there may not even be a place there."

Mary thought for a moment. It had been a long, hard journey and she was exhausted. Sweat was still glistening on the donkey's back, and Mary felt an ache in her side from the long ride. She desperately needed to rest. Going back to Jerusalem would take over an hour, and they would have to spend another hour returning the next day for the census. "I'm willing to put up with it if you are," she told Joseph. "It's only for one night."

So Mary and Joseph reluctantly trudged to the back of the inn where they entered the cavelike stable. It was dusty and dark and thick with the stench of animals. A donkey brayed, breaking the silence. The young couple decided to bed down in the city of Bethlehem, unaware of the prophecy they were about to fulfill.

Prophecy of Jesus' Birth

The Old Testament clearly prophesied the city in which the Messiah would be born.

> But you, Bethlehem Ephrathah, though you are small among the clans of Judah, out of you will come for me one who will be ruler over Israel, whose origins are from of old, from ancient times (Micah 5:2).

There are several important aspects of this prophecy.

1. Bethlehem was small—too small to be counted among the cities of Judah (note its absence in Joshua 15:48-60).

2. The "ruler of Israel" will have origins "of old, from ancient times." This implies the eternal preexistence of Jesus (as indicated in John 1).

3. The correct Bethlehem was specified—Bethlehem *Ephrathah*—Ephrathah is similar to a "county." There was a second Bethlehem close to Nazareth.

Fulfillment

"After Jesus was born in Bethlehem in Judea..." (Matthew 2:1). What are the odds of this prophecy randomly coming true? Some scholars estimate the population of Palestine was approximately 209,000 at the time, and the population of Bethlehem from 2,000 to 4,200. Hence, there would be only one or two chances in a hundred that the Messiah would be born in Bethlehem—if only the population of Palestine were considered.

However, why wouldn't the entire world be considered? In such a case, we need to consider the population of Bethlehem versus the population of the world—estimated to be about 300 million at the time. In such a case, the odds of the Messiah being born in Bethlehem are about 1 in 100,000,000!

Jesus' birth in Bethlehem, fulfilling the messianic prophecy, is a strong indication of divine planning and intervention as indicated in the Bible.

Prophecy of Jesus' Ancestors

The Old Testament clearly defines the Messiah's ancestors. Incredibly they precisely define the ancestors of Jesus.

Prophecy	Fulfillment
Abraham — "...Your descendants will take possession of the cities of their enemies and through your offspring all nations on earth will be blessed, because you have obeyed me" (Genesis 22:17-18).	**Fulfillment** — "The promises were spoken to Abraham and to his seed. The Scripture does not say 'and to seeds,' meaning many people, but 'and to your seed,' meaning one person, who is Christ" (Galatians 3:16).
Isaac — "...because it is through Isaac that your offspring will be reckoned (Genesis 21:12).	**Fulfillment** — "He was...the son of Isaac" (Luke 3:23,34).

Prophecy	Fulfillment
Jacob — "I see him, but not now; I behold him, but not near. A star will come out of Jacob; a scepter will rise out of Israel" (Numbers 24:17).	**Fulfillment** — "He was…the son of Jacob" (Luke 3:23,34).
Judah — "The scepter will not depart from Judah, nor the ruler's staff from between his feet, until he comes to whom it belongs and the obedience of the nations is his" (Genesis 49:10).	**Fulfillment** — "He was…the son of Judah" (Luke 3:23,33).
Jesse — "A shoot will come up from the stump of Jesse; from his roots a Branch will bear fruit. The Spirit of the LORD will rest on him" (Isaiah 11:1-2).	**Fulfillment** — "He was…the son of Jesse" (Luke 3:23,32).
David — "'The days are coming,' declares the LORD, 'when I will raise up to David a righteous Branch, a King who will reign wisely and do what is just and right in the land'" (Jeremiah 23:5).	**Fulfillment** — "He was…son of David" (Luke 3:23,31).

The prophecies of Jesus' ancestors—all irrefutably verified in the Old Testament hundreds of years in advance—are by themselves significant evidence of supernatural involvement in placing a specific person, Jesus, on earth. What are the odds of all of these prophecies existing by accident? Let's make the following assumptions based on population estimates of the world.[1]

Abraham—one chance in 15 million (population of the world's men).

Isaac—one chance in 2 (Abraham had only two sons).

Jacob—one chance in 2 (Isaac had only two sons).

Judah—one chance in 12 (Jacob had only twelve sons).

Jesse—one chance in 240 (Judah had 5 sons, Perez had at least 2 sons, Hezron had 3 sons, Ram had 4 sons, Amminadab had at least 1 son, Nahshon had at least 1 son, Salmon had at least 1 son, Boaz had at least 1 son, Obed had at least 2 sons (5 x 2 x 3 x 4 x 1 x 1 x 1 x 1 x 2 = 240).

David—one chance in 8.

Total odds of randomly *finding prophecies* for all of the above ancestors (that were also fulfilled in one man) without supernatural intervention is about 15,000,000 x 2 x 2 x 12 x 240 x 8 = 1,382,400,000,000! One chance in 1.3824 trillion.

A Unique Twist to the Prophecies of Jesus' Ancestors

The prophet Jeremiah prophesied that Jehoiachin, an evil king and descendent of David, was cursed by God and would never inherit the throne of David:

"As surely as I live," declares the LORD, "even if you, Jehoiachin son of Jehoiakim king of Judah, were a signet ring on my right hand, I would still pull you off. I will hand you over to those who seek your life, those you fear—to Nebuchadnezzar king of Babylon and to the Babylonians. I will hurl you and the mother who gave you birth into another country, where neither of you was born, and there you both will die. You will never come back to the land you long to return to."

Is this man Jehoiachin a despised, broken pot, an object no one wants? Why will he and his children be hurled out, cast into a land they do not know? O land, land, land, hear the word of the Lord! This is what the Lord says: "Record this man as if childless, a man who will not prosper in his lifetime, for none of his offspring will prosper, none will sit on the throne of David or rule anymore in Judah" (Jeremiah 22:24-30).

So the question becomes, How can this prophecy be fulfilled—that no child of Jehoiachin would inherit David's throne—(since Jeremiah is speaking for God) if Jesus is the Messiah and descends through the line of David?

The answer is that Jesus descended from the line of David both from his mother's side (Luke 3:23-31) and also on his father's side (Matthew 1:6-16). The "right" of kingship carried forward through Joseph (the male side). However Joseph was not the natural parent of Jesus. The real father of Jesus was the Holy Spirit:

> "Do not be afraid, Mary, you have found favor with God. You will be with child and give birth to a son, and you are to give him the name Jesus. He will be great and will be called the Son of the Most High. The Lord God will give him the throne of his father David, and he will reign over the house of Jacob forever; his kingdom will never end."
>
> "How will this be," Mary asked the angel, "since I am a virgin?"
>
> The angel answered, "The Holy Spirit will come upon you, and the power of the Most High will overshadow you. So the holy one to be born will be called the Son of God" (Luke 1:30-36).

God fulfilled the prophecy of Jeremiah by having Joseph's son be conceived by the Holy Spirit, while still affording Jesus the "right of kingship" by having Joseph as his legal father.

The prophecy of Jesus' ancestors alone is strong evidence of supernatural involvement in defining the Messianic role, as indicated in the Bible.

Prophecy of the "Passing of the Scepter"

The book of Genesis provides the important Messianic prophecy regarding the scepter of control by God's chosen people, the Jews: "The scepter will not depart from Judah, nor the ruler's staff from between his feet, until he comes to whom it belongs and the obedience of the nations is his" (Genesis 49:10).

The Jews regarded this prophecy as extremely significant. It was a promise that they would maintain control of their laws until the Messiah arrived. However, when the Romans usurped the Law of Moses by forbidding them to carry out the ultimate sentence for blasphemy (death by stoning), it was regarded as the passing of the scepter. This happened in about A.D. 11 when Archelaus, son and successor of Herod, was deposed.[2]

Note that even during captivity in Babylon, the Jews maintained judicial authority. For this prophecy and others to be fulfilled, the following had to happen:

1. The Messiah had to be born before the scepter being passed (before A.D. 11).

2. The death of the Messiah had to happen after the passing of the scepter, since other prophecy indicated the death would be by crucifixion, not stoning as was the penalty prior to the passing of the scepter.

These two requirements allowed only a very brief time period for the Messiah to be born, to live, and to be executed by crucifixion.

Jesus fulfilled these two criteria by being born sometime from 7 B.C. to 2 B.C. (scholars dispute the date, although the most commonly accepted date is 4 B.C.). Furthermore, Jesus was crucified sometime around A.D. 32, fulfilling the second criterion.

What are the odds of this prophecy being fulfilled by accident? We must consider fulfillment to be within the lifespan of an individual (because he would have to be born prior to the scepter being passed and die after it being passed). First, we might assume a lifespan of 70 years. Second, we might consider all of the time from today back to the time of Abraham to be about 4,000 years. Hence there would be about 57 generations of 70 years in which the prophecy could be fulfilled. So the odds of random fulfillment without God would be about one chance in 57.

Yet this needs to also coincide with death by crucifixion and other prophecies that dramatically reduce the random possibility of this prophecy coming true. As a result, we might conclude that fulfillment of the precise date in prophecy for the birth of the Messiah both supports the biblical claims and adds to the likelihood of divine fulfillment.

Prophecy of Being "Called Out of Egypt"

Old Testament Prophecy

An Old Testament prophecy reads: "When Israel was a child, I loved him, and out of Egypt I called my son" (Hosea 11:1).

Fulfillment in the New Testament

The New Testament gives an account of the fulfillment of the prophecy, and it further indicates that an angel of the Lord appeared to Jesus' parents and told them to flee to Egypt to avoid an impending slaughter by Herod:

> When they had gone, an angel of the Lord appeared to Joseph in a dream. "Get up," he said, "take

the child and his mother and escape to Egypt. Stay there until I tell you, for Herod is going to search for the child to kill him."

So he got up, took the child and his mother during the night and left for Egypt, where he stayed until the death of Herod. *And so was fulfilled what the Lord had said through the prophet: "Out of Egypt I called my son."*

When Herod realized that he had been outwitted by the Magi, he was furious, and he gave orders to kill all the boys in Bethlehem and its vicinity who were two years old and under, in accordance with the time he had learned from the Magi. Then what was said through the prophet Jeremiah was fulfilled: "A voice is heard in Ramah, weeping and great mourning, Rachel weeping for her children and refusing to be comforted, because they are no more."

After Herod died, an angel of the Lord appeared in a dream to Joseph in Egypt and said, "Get up, take the child and his mother and go to the land of Israel, for those who were trying to take the child's life are dead" (Matthew 2:13-20).

What are the odds that—

1. there would be an accurate prophecy, hundreds of years in advance, about a Messiah (God's Son) coming "out of Egypt"?

2. there would be an angel who would prophesy of impending doom of the slaughter of children?

3. the Herod slaughter would occur precisely as predicted?

Since these prophecies involve supernatural events (God's Son and an angel), any chance of random fulfillment would be virtually zero without divine intervention.

Prophecy That Jesus Would Perform Special Miracles

Prophecy

The Old Testament prophesied that a Messiah would come who would perform miracles that were only attributable to God:

> "Be strong, do not fear; your God will come, he will come with vengeance; with divine retribution he will come to save you."
> Then will the eyes of the blind be opened and the ears of the deaf unstopped. Then will the lame leap like a deer, and the mute tongue shout for joy (Isaiah 35:4-6).

Fulfillment

> Then he went up on a mountainside and sat down. Great crowds came to him, bringing the lame, the blind, the crippled, the mute and many others, and laid them at his feet; and he healed them (Matthew 15:29-30).

What are the chances of this prophecy being fulfilled without divine intervention? Essentially zero since we are dealing with supernatural events. Virtually nobody has been seriously considered to have the ability to do such healing on a routine, dependable basis. Jesus is unique.

The skeptic might claim that this was a contrived prophecy by Christians, and that the special miracles by Jesus never happened. However, Jesus' miracles are not uniquely claimed in the Bible. Non-Christian references at the time of the eyewitnesses and shortly thereafter recorded them as well (see chapter 10).

We can conclude that Jesus' fulfillment of the prophecy that the Messiah would perform healing attributed only to God is strong support of his claim to be God, as stated in the Bible.

Prophecy That Jesus Would Speak in Parables

During his ministry, Jesus' disciples were puzzled why he often spoke in parables. The Bible records their question and Jesus' response this way:

> The disciples came to him and asked, "Why do you speak to the people in parables?"
>
> He replied, "The knowledge of the secrets of the kingdom of heaven has been given to you, but not to them. Whoever has will be given more, and he will have an abundance. Whoever does not have, even what he has will be taken from him. This is why I speak to them in parables: "Though seeing, they do not see; though hearing, they do not hear or understand" (Matthew 13:10-13).

Interestingly, a psalmist prophesied hundreds of years in advance that the Messiah would speak in parables: "I will open my mouth in parables, I will utter hidden things, things from of old" (Psalm 78:2).

Sometimes people are confused by Jesus' response to his disciples. His answer does not mean that parables were given to "hide" the message. In fact, it was often easier to understand via a story than otherwise. Instead, it meant that the doctrine taught in parables was new teaching that had not yet been understood by the great body of Jews (either intentionally or unintentionally).

THE PARABLES OF JESUS

The Kingdom of God

1. The Soils (Matthew 13:3-8; Mark 4:3-8; Luke 8:5-8)
2. The Weeds (Matthew 13:24-30)

3. The Mustard Seed (Matthew 13:31-32; Mark 4:30-32; Luke 13:18-19)

4. The Yeast (Matthew 13:33; Luke 13:20-21)

5. The Treasure (Matthew 13:44)

6. The Pearl (Matthew 13:45-46)

7. The Fishing Net (Matthew 13:47-50)

8. The Wheat (Mark 4:26-29)

Service and Obedience

9. The Workers in the Harvest (Matthew 20:1-16)

10. The Entrusted Money (Matthew 25:14-30)

11. The Servants' Investments (Luke 19:11-27)

12. The Servant's Role (Luke 17:7-10)

Prayer

13. The Friend at Midnight (Luke 11:5-10)

14. The Unjust Judge (Luke 18:1-8)

Neighbors

15. The Good Samaritan (Luke 10:30-37)

Humility

16. The Wedding Feast (Luke 14:7-11)

17. The Pharisee and the Tax Collector (Luke 18:9-14)

Wealth

18. The Rich Fool (Luke 12:16-21)

19. The Great Feast (Luke 14:16-24)

20. The Shrewd Manager (Luke 16:1-9)

God's Love

21. The Lost Sheep (Matthew 18:12-14; Luke 15:3-7)

22. The Lost Coin (Luke 15:8-10)

23. The Lost Son (Luke 15:11-32)

Thankfulness

24. The Forgiven Debts (Luke 7:41-43)

Christ's Return

25. The Ten Virgins (Matthew 25:1-13)

26. The Wise and Faithful Servant (Matthew 24:45-51; Luke 12:42-48)

27. The Traveling Owner of the House (Mark 13:34-37)

God's Values

28. The Two Sons (Matthew 21:28-32)

29. The Wicked Tenants (Matthew 21:33-41; Mark 12:1-9; Luke 20:9-16)

30. The Fig Tree (Luke 13:6-9)

31. The Marriage Feast (Matthew 22:1-14)

32. The Unforgiving Servant (Matthew 18:23-35)

The prophecy that the Messiah would speak in parables was fulfilled by Jesus and is one more piece of evidence that he is the Messiah.

CONCLUSION

As demonstrated, the odds against any of these prophecies coming true are quite extraordinary. The odds of them all coming true in one person is essentially impossible without divine intervention. This indicates that Jesus indeed fulfilled the requirements for the biblical Messiah.

Prophecies Leading Up to Jesus' Crucifixion

The morning air was crisp with a remaining hint of dew. Already the sun was casting sharp shadows of a glorious day yet to come. Slowly the small group ambled down the rocky slope on the Mount of Olives toward the city of Jerusalem. Jesus had mounted a donkey and his disciples trailed behind. The donkey slipped a little on a damp rock as it walked down a steep portion of the slope, making a turn toward the city. Suddenly a throng of people came into view. At the appearance of Jesus they immediately broke out in joyful cheers and shouts:

"Blessed is the king who comes in the name of the Lord!"
"Peace in heaven and glory in the highest!" (Luke 19:38).

The disciples were especially excited because this was the first time Jesus allowed them to proclaim him as king.

The crowd was intensely rejoicing, and at times crowded too close to the band of men trying to make it into the city. In the back of the crowd stood the Pharisees and Sadducees in solemn, stern judgment of the scene before them.

"Teacher, rebuke your disciples!" scolded the Pharisees when they heard the cheers (Luke 19:39). But Jesus knew that this was his day...the day that was precisely foretold more than 500 years before by the prophet Daniel. Jesus knew that even if the crowd was silenced the stones would cry out!

ARGUABLY THE MOST AMAZING PROPHECY in the Bible is the prophecy of the exact day in which Jesus allowed himself to be called king—his entry into Jerusalem days before his crucifixion (now called Palm Sunday). The prophet Daniel was in the midst of praying when Gabriel (the angel that announces great things such as the birth of Jesus) came to him with an announcement. The prophecy is seemingly cryptic and requires some understanding:

> "Seventy 'sevens' are decreed for your people and your holy city to finish transgression, to put an end to sin, to atone for wickedness, to bring in everlasting righteousness, to seal up vision and prophecy and to anoint the most holy.
>
> "Know and understand this: From the issuing of the decree to restore and rebuild Jerusalem until the Anointed One, the ruler, comes, there will be seven 'sevens,' and sixty-two 'sevens.' It will be rebuilt with streets and a trench, but in times of trouble. After the sixty-two 'sevens,' the Anointed One will be cut off and will have nothing. The people of the ruler who will come will destroy the city and the sanctuary. The end will come like a flood: War will continue until the end, and desolations have been decreed. He will confirm a covenant with many for one 'seven.' In the middle of

the 'seven' he will put an end to sacrifice and offering. And on a wing [of the temple] he will set up an abomination that causes desolation, until the end that is decreed is poured out on him" (Daniel 9:24-27, brackets in original).

The four essential points in this prophecy are:

1. The first seven "sevens" or 49 years, is the length of time for something (perhaps completion of the restoration and rebuilding of Jerusalem?).

2. A total of 69 periods of "seven" (7 + 62) will pass from the decree to rebuild Jerusalem until the coming of the "Anointed One" (Messiah, in Hebrew). This dates Jesus' entry into Jerusalem.

3. After that time the Anointed One will be cut off (Hebrew: *yikaret,* meaning a sudden, violent end—the crucifixion).

4. And after that time the city and the temple will be destroyed.

The "periods of seven" could be expressed in days or years. (*Note:* Evidence earlier in the chapter of Daniel and elsewhere suggests that this prophecy is based on "sevens" of years.) The starting point for this prophecy is the decree by Artaxerxes to rebuild Jerusalem given on March 5, 444 B.C. (the first day of the month of Nisan that year—Nehemiah 2:1-6).

The First "Seven"

We find two interesting historical facts regarding the first "seven sevens" or 49 years indicated in the prophecy (Daniel 9:25). 1) It took 49 years to restore Jerusalem, 2) additionally, 49 years after 444 B.C., the Old Testament canon (completed with Malachi) was entirely written.

69 "Sevens"

Adding the seven "sevens" with the 62 "sevens" we come up with 69 "sevens." Calculating this based on the standard Jewish prophetic year of 360 days, we arrive at a total of 173,880 days from the day of the decree until the arrival of the Anointed One. The question becomes, Does this number of days correspond to the day that Jesus entered Jerusalem on a donkey?

The number of actual days from the decree by Artaxerxes until the Anointed One arrives is in "real time" not "prophetic time." The difference between 444 B.C. and A.D. 33 is 476 "solar" years (note: there is no year zero). We know that there are 365 days, 5 hours, 48 minutes, and 45.975 seconds in a solar year. Multiplying 476 solar years by 365.242198 we come to 173,855 days. Hence, there is a difference of 25 days between the prophetic "years" in Daniel's prophecy and the actual solar "years" from 444 B.C. to A.D. 33 assuming a "date" of March 5 in each year. However, the Jewish lunar year differs annually from the solar year of the Julian calendar.

To coordinate the two, it would be necessary to take the starting point of March 5, 444 B.C. and add 173,855 days to bring it to the same solar date in A.D. 33 (i.e., March 5). To arrive at the prophetic date, 25 days need to be added, bringing it to March 30, A.D. 33. Does this have any significance, using the Jewish calendar, in relationship to Jesus' entry into Jerusalem?

Yes. In A.D. 33, March 30 marked the tenth of Nisan on the Jewish calendar. This would have been the date of the triumphal entry, or the entry into Jerusalem on Palm Sunday.[1] The Passover lamb was selected on the tenth of Nisan, which would have been the day that Jesus entered Jerusalem ("selected" by a rejoicing crowd) as the ultimate Passover lamb prior to his crucifixion.[2] Hence, the prophecy precisely predicts the day Jesus entered Jerusalem allowing himself to be called king!

The Crucifixion

As prophesied, Jesus did experience a sudden, "violent end" after his entry as the Anointed One—his crucifixion.

Destruction of the City and Temple

As prophesied, the city of Jerusalem and the temple were completely destroyed by the Romans in A.D. 70.

What are the odds of these prophecies being fulfilled without divine intervention? There have been over 923,000 days available for fulfillment of this prophecy since Daniel made it. Hence, the odds are about one in 923,000 for the timing issue alone! The other prophecy elements add to the unlikelihood of coincidence.

In summary, this remarkable prophecy of the exact day of Jesus' entry into Jerusalem as the Anointed One, along with the other prophecies in Daniel 9, provide compelling evidence of Jesus' role as the Messiah, precisely as indicated in the Bible.

Prophecy of a King on a Donkey

Leaders in ancient times, especially kings, never rode donkeys. Donkeys were regarded as appropriate only for peasants and the lower class. However Zechariah made it clear more than 500 years before Jesus, that the Messiah would arrive, allowing himself to be called king for the first time, riding on a donkey:

> Rejoice greatly, O Daughter of Zion!
> Shout, Daughter of Jerusalem!
> See, your king comes to you,
> righteous and having salvation,
> gentle and riding on a donkey,
> on a colt, the foal of a donkey (Zechariah 9:9).

What are the odds of this event happening by chance? Extremely remote. Skeptics could argue that it was Jesus' intention to fulfill the Messianic prophecy and might argue that he chose to do it for that purpose alone. Such an argument, however, must be evaluated in light of all other prophecies that uniquely fit Jesus as well. True, some might be purposely fulfilled by Jesus, but most could not. The odds of all of them coming true in one person are far beyond human reasoning.

Prophecies of Jesus' Betrayal

There are several specific details provided in Old Testament prophecy about the actual betrayal of Jesus.

Prophecy

1. Betrayal by a friend

> Even my close friend, whom I trusted, he who shared my bread, has lifted up his heel against me (Psalm 41:9).

Fulfillment

> Then one of the Twelve—the one called Judas Iscariot—went to the chief priests and asked, "What are you willing to give me if I hand him over to you?" So they counted out for him thirty silver coins. From then on Judas watched for an opportunity to hand him over (Matthew 26:14-16).

> After he had said this, Jesus was troubled in spirit and testified, "I tell you the truth, one of you is going to betray me." His disciples stared at one another, at a loss to know which one of them he meant. One of them, the disciple whom Jesus loved, was reclining next to him. Simon Peter motioned to this disciple and said, "Ask him which one he means." Leaning back against

Jesus, he asked him, "Lord, who is it?" Jesus answered, "It is the one to whom I will give this piece of bread when I have dipped it in the dish." Then, dipping the piece of bread, he gave it to Judas Iscariot, son of Simon. As soon as Judas took the bread, Satan entered into him. "What you are about to do, do quickly," Jesus told him, but no one at the meal understood why Jesus said this to him (John 13:21-28).

Prophecy

2. Betrayal for 30 pieces of silver, thrown on the Temple floor, and given to a potter

It was revoked on that day, and so the afflicted of the flock who were watching me knew it was the word of the LORD.

I told them, "If you think it best, give me my pay; but if not, keep it." So they paid me *thirty pieces of silver.*

And the LORD said to me, *"Throw it to the potter"*—the handsome price at which they priced me! So I took the thirty pieces of silver and *threw them into the house of the LORD to the potter* (Zechariah 11:11-13).

Fulfillment

Then one of the Twelve—the one called Judas Iscariot—went to the chief priests and asked, "What are you willing to give me if I hand him over to you?" So they counted out for him *thirty silver coins.* From then on Judas watched for an opportunity to hand him over (Matthew 26:14-16).

So Judas *threw the money into the temple* and left. Then he went away and hanged himself (Matthew 27:5).

The chief priests picked up the coins and said, "It is against the law to put this into the treasury, since it is blood money." So they decided to use the money *to buy the potter's field* as a burial place for foreigners. That is why it has been called the Field of Blood to this day. Then what was spoken by Jeremiah the prophet was fulfilled: "They took the *thirty silver coins,* the price set on him by the people of Israel, and they used them to buy *the potter's field,* as the Lord commanded me" (Matthew 27:6-10).

Could all these prophecies come true without divine intervention? Being betrayed by a friend was, perhaps, not so unusual at the time. But arriving at exactly 30 pieces of silver seems a bit more unlikely. Then there is the throwing of the money onto the Temple floor. First, the perpetrator would need to feel remorse. Second, he would need such remorse as to not want the money. Third, he would have to decide to throw it into the Temple—an odd choice.

Using the money to purchase a potter's field is also very unique. Even though the chief priests were faced with a dilemma of what to do with the blood money (that couldn't be used for the Temple), the chances of them deciding upon buying a field owned by a potter was slim.

The prophesied details of the betrayal of Jesus provide substantial evidence that he was the Messiah as described in the Bible.

Prophecy of Silence at Jesus' Trial

Jesus said nothing to defend himself at one of his trials. This was highly unusual. In fact, Jesus only spoke in answer to questions:

> Then the high priest stood up and said to Jesus, "Are you not going to answer? What is this testimony that these men are bringing against you?" But Jesus remained silent.
>
> The high priest said to him, "I charge you under oath by the living God: Tell us if you are the Christ, the Son of God."

"Yes, it is as you say," Jesus replied. "But I say to all of you: In the future you will see the Son of Man sitting at the right hand of the Mighty One and coming on the clouds of heaven" (Matthew 26:62-64).

The Old Testament prophesied that Jesus would remain silent when accused by false witnesses:

He was oppressed and afflicted, yet he did not open his mouth; he was led like a lamb to the slaughter, and as a sheep before her shearers is silent, so he did not open his mouth (Isaiah 53:7).

Skeptics could argue that Jesus was deranged and, having a "messiah complex," wanted to fulfill the prophecies of the Messiah. But this is unlikely. And Jesus would certainly know there were many other prophecies that had to be fulfilled that he couldn't control.

In analyzing the probability of Jesus remaining silent, we cannot relate it to today's court of law, where people frequently plead the Fifth Amendment. Jesus had no attorney skillfully directing his defense. The entire defense rested upon his words of rebuttal. The fact that Jesus didn't defend himself even though he was innocent fulfilled prophecy and shows that Jesus was the Messiah described in the Bible.

Prophecy of False Witnesses at Jesus' Trial

Prophecy

The Old Testament indicates that the Messiah would endure accusations by false witnesses:

Do not turn me over to the desire of my foes, for false witnesses rise up against me, breathing out violence (Psalm 27:12).

Fulfillment

> The chief priests and the whole Sanhedrin were looking for false evidence against Jesus so that they could put him to death. But they did not find any, though many false witnesses came forward (Matthew 26:59-60).

Prophecy of Being Lifted Up Like a Snake in the Desert

The Old Testament contains models or "types" that are a form of prophecy about other people and events. An example of such a "type" is the account of how God wanted Moses to deal with the venomous snakes that caused death in the desert during the Exodus:

> Then the LORD sent venomous snakes among them; they bit the people and many Israelites died. The people came to Moses and said, "We sinned when we spoke against the LORD and against you. Pray that the LORD will take the snakes away from us." So Moses prayed for the people.
>
> The LORD said to Moses, "Make a snake and put it up on a pole; anyone who is bitten can look at it and live." So Moses made a bronze snake and put it up on a pole. Then when anyone was bitten by a snake and looked at the bronze snake, he lived (Numbers 21:6-9).

Here we see several essential prophetic points:

1. The "picture" of snakes being the cause of death. Snakes are symbolic of Satan throughout the Bible, and Satan is the "prince of death."

2. Sin is responsible for death (see Romans 6:23).

3. The bronze snake was lifted on a pole, similar to Jesus being lifted on a cross. Both offered people a chance to be saved from death caused by sin.

4. People still had to "look to the snake raised on a pole" to be saved. Today, people still have to "look to Jesus" by believing in him to be saved.

The parallel between the two situations is obvious to any objective observer.

Prophecy of Crucifixion

Three times the Old Testament prophesied about the crucifixion of Jesus:

1. David wrote the well-known "Crucifixion Psalm" in about 1000 B.C.—"They have pierced my hands and my feet" (Psalm 22:16).

2. Isaiah wrote the famous chapter 53—circa 700 B.C.—it's an accurate description of Jesus—"But he was pierced for our transgressions, he was crushed for our iniquities" (Isaiah 53:5).

3. Zechariah in about 500 B.C.—"And I will pour out on the house of David and the inhabitants of Jerusalem a spirit of grace and supplication. They will look on me, the one they have pierced, and they will mourn for him as one mourns for an only child, and grieve bitterly for him as one grieves for a firstborn son" (Zechariah 12:10-11).

Crucifixion was not even invented by the Romans until about 400 B.C.! Isn't it amazing that there were three prophecies that the Messiah would be pierced (crucified) hundreds of years before that method of execution had even been devised? The skeptic might say the Scripture says "pierced" not crucified, but this is probably because there was no word for it yet!

In summary, prophecies of the crucifixion of Jesus centuries before the method had been devised is strong evidence that he was the Messiah as indicated in the Bible.

Prophecy of Rejection

Jesus taught his disciples the truth about what was about to happen:

> If the world hates you, keep in mind that it hated me first. If you belonged to the world, it would love you as its own. As it is, you do not belong to the world, but I have chosen you out of the world. That is why the world hates you. Remember the words I spoke to you: "No servant is greater than his master." If they persecuted me, they will persecute you also. If they obeyed my teaching, they will obey yours also. They will treat you this way because of my name, for they do not know the One who sent me. If I had not come and spoken to them, they would not be guilty of sin. Now, however, they have no excuse for their sin. He who hates me hates my Father as well. If I had not done among them what no one else did, they would not be guilty of sin. But now they have seen these miracles, and yet they have hated both me and my Father. But this is to fulfill what is written in their Law: "They hated me without reason" (John 15:18-25).

The Old Testament also prophesied that the Messiah would be hated without cause:

> Let not those gloat over me who are my enemies without cause; let not those who hate me without reason maliciously wink the eye (Psalm 35:19).

> The stone the builders rejected has become the capstone; the LORD has done this, and it is marvelous in our eyes (Psalm 118:22-23).

What are the odds of the Messiah coincidentally being rejected without cause? It is not especially significant; however, it does add to the long list of fulfilled prophecies. In summary, Jesus was rejected just as the ancient prophecies predicted.

ONCLUSION

We see a mounting list of remarkable and precise prophecies about Jesus that add substantial evidence that Jesus is the Son of God.

Prophecies About Jesus' Crucifixion and Resurrection

The traders trudged along the winding road toward the hill outside the glorious city of Jerusalem. It was an especially important time for them to visit the city because the Passover pilgrims always seemed in a good mood to spend money. This year the traders were late, missing the critical selling week prior to the Passover itself. Oh well, there was still a week left of celebration and plenty of time to sell. In the distance they could hear sounds of laughter, and they could make out the form they knew all too well—the image of crosses on a hill. No doubt the Romans had crucified some thieves.

As they approached the scene, the laughter increased, almost to a fever pitch. People were merciless in the mocking of one of the crucified victims; someone named Jesus. The traders wondered what horrible crime he had committed to deserve such disgrace beyond his final deadly humiliation.

Finally they arrived beneath the cross of Jesus. Some soldiers were gambling for his clothes. Even one of the thieves on the cross was mocking him. One of the traders looked up at the face of the one so critically attacked. Surprisingly, Jesus didn't have the hardened face of a criminal at all. Looking into his eyes, the trader sensed an awareness, a peace, an unmistakable love. "Hmmm," thought the trader, "it doesn't seem to be the kind of face one would mock."

Prophecy

David's Crucifixion Psalm (Psalm 22) prophesies Jesus' experience on the cross and describes the comments of passers by:

> All who see me mock me; they hurl insults, shaking their heads: "He trusts in the LORD; let the LORD rescue him (Psalm 22:7-8).

Fulfillment

> Two robbers were crucified with him, one on his right and one on his left. Those who passed by hurled insults at him, shaking their heads and saying, "You who are going to destroy the temple and build it in three days, save yourself! Come down from the cross, if you are the Son of God!" (Matthew 27:38-40).

> In the same way the chief priests, the teachers of the law and the elders mocked him (Matthew 27:41).

> In the same way the robbers who were crucified with him also heaped insults on him (Matthew 27:44).

The fulfillment of the prophecy that Jesus would be mocked is surprising. Without divine intervention, we would normally assume that anyone worthy of being a Messiah would not warrant mocking.

Prophecy of Casting Lots for His Clothing

Prophecy

The Old Testament prophesied about the casting of lots for the Messiah's clothing: "They divide my garments among them and cast lots for my clothing" (Psalm 22:18).

Fulfillment

> Dividing up his clothes, they cast lots to see what each would get (Mark 15:24).

It's highly unlikely that anyone, let alone the Messiah, would have garments gambled away by others. The fulfillment of this prophecy beats the odds by a long shot.

Prophecy of Being Assigned a Grave with Thieves

His head hung down with the weight of a millstone. His breathing was labored...very labored. Jesus didn't know how much longer he could survive. Behind him to his left he heard a long cry of deep anguish. One thief began to scoff at Jesus:

> Aren't you the Christ? Save yourself and us! (Luke 23:39).

Jesus' heart was heavy with the burden he was enduring. The other thief pushed up on the spikes in his feet for a deep breath and moaned,

> "Don't you fear God," he said, "since you are under the same sentence? We are punished justly, for we are getting what our deeds deserve. But this man has done nothing wrong."
> Then he said, "Jesus, remember me when you come into your kingdom."

> Jesus answered him, "I tell you the truth, today you
> will be with me in paradise" (Luke 23:40-43).

The Old Testament prophesied that the Messiah would be assaigned a grave with thieves: "He was assigned a grave with the wicked" (Isaiah 53:9).

Because Jesus was executed with two thieves, he was assigned a grave with the wicked.

Certainly nobody would expect the Messiah to be assigned a grave with thieves. The probability that such a prophecy would randomly come true is extremely remote.

Prophecy of Being Given a Grave with the Rich

Prophecy

The Old Testament prophesied that the Messiah, though assigned a grave with the wicked, would actually be given a grave with the rich upon his death: "He was assigned a grave with the wicked, and with the rich in his death" (Isaiah 53:9).

Fulfillment

> As evening approached, there came a rich man
> from Arimathea, named Joseph, who had himself
> become a disciple of Jesus. Going to Pilate, he asked for
> Jesus' body, and Pilate ordered that it be given to him.
> Joseph took the body, wrapped it in a clean linen cloth,
> and placed it in his own new tomb that he had cut out
> of the rock (Matthew 27:57-60).

This prophecy by itself is not unusual; it is the combination of being assigned a grave with the wicked and buried with the rich that makes it unique. However, Jesus was from a peasant family so it does seem strange that he was buried in a rich man's tomb.

Prophecy That No Bones Would Be Broken

Prophecy

The Old Testament prophesied that no bones would be broken in the Messiah: "…He protects all his bones, not one of them will be broken" (Psalm 34:20).

Fulfillment

> But when they came to Jesus and found that he was already dead, they did not break his legs (John 19:33).

> These things happened so that the scripture would be fulfilled: "Not one of his bones will be broken" (John 19:36).

With a crucifixion, legs were often broken in order to hasten death by suffocation. It was quite unlikely that this fulfillment would be due to coincidence.

Prophecy That the Messiah's Heart Would Fail

Prophecy

The Crucifixion Psalm in the Old Testament prophesied that the Messiah's heart would fail: "My heart has turned to wax; it has melted away within me" (Psalm 22:14).

Fulfillment

> Instead, one of the soldiers pierced Jesus' side with a spear, bringing a sudden flow of blood and water (John 19:34-35).

In a crucifixion, death is almost always by asphyxiation. In Jesus' case, though, the blood and water from the spear wound indicate probable heart failure.

Prophecy That the Messiah's Body Will Not See Decay

Prophecy

The Old Testament boldly prophesied that the Messiah would not see decay: "…Nor will you let your Holy One see decay" (Psalm 16:10).

Fulfillment

The resurrection of Jesus, of course, would preclude decay.

> But God raised him from the dead, freeing him from the agony of death, because it was impossible for death to keep its hold on him (Acts 2:24).

> …because you will not abandon me to the grave, nor will you let your Holy One see decay (Acts 2:27).

What are the odds of someone coincidentally fulfilling this messianic prophecy? Coincidence is *impossible* without a resurrection. What are the odds of a resurrection? Virtually zero without divine intervention.

Prophecy that the Messiah would not see decay only fits Jesus' resurrection and is strong evidence of his fulfilling the Messianic role outlined in the Bible.

Probability of Prophecies About Jesus

The Bible teaches us to "test everything" and hold on to the truth (1 Thessalonians 5:21). Furthermore, the Bible teaches us that the one test that sets God apart from everything is 100 percent perfectly fulfilled prophecy:

> I am God, and there is no other; I am God, and there is none like me. I make known the end from the beginning, from ancient times, what is still to come (Isaiah 46:9-10).

> If what a prophet proclaims in the name of the LORD does not take place or come true, that is a message the LORD has not spoken. That prophet has spoken presumptuously. Do not be afraid of him (Deuteronomy 18:22).

> But a prophet who presumes to speak in my name anything I have not commanded him to say, or a prophet who speaks in the name of other gods, must be put to death (Deuteronomy 18:20).

Fulfilled prophecy was (and is) the primary test of something being from God. It is used extensively throughout the Bible.

The probability of the Old Testament prophecies of the Messiah all coming true in one person is far beyond reason. Understanding the enormous unlikelihood of winning a typical state lottery helps us realize just how impossible such a coincidence is. We have just broken down 35 distinct prophecies of Jesus. We also saw that some were "impossible" prophecies (e.g., the resurrection necessary for "there to be no decay") and others that were extremely remote (e.g., the odds of prophesying the precise date of Jesus' triumphal entry—nearly one chance in 1,000,000).

However, to be extremely conservative, let's assume that each prophecy had 1 chance in only 10 of being coincidental. It still would mean that the odds of all coming true would equal one chance in 10^{35}. This would be like winning five state lotteries in a row with a single ticket for each! This would be like guessing a single second out of 15 billion years—not once, but twice! Imagine how much more incredible this would be if realistic odds (instead of 1 chance in 10) were used.

One can easily see why prophecy is a test of something being from God since "only God knows the end from the beginning." (Coincidentally guessing all these prophecies would, obviously, be impossible.)

The prophecies outlined in this and the previous chapters are not all of the Messianic prophesies contained in the Old Testament. Even so, they provide ample evidence to demonstrate statistically that God clearly had a hand in determining the Messiah, and that the only realistic candidate is Jesus of Nazareth.

CONCLUSION

As the Bible indicates, we can and should "test everything," and we should test the inspiration by God using 100 percent perfectly fulfilled prophecy. With this test, we find that Jesus is without question the Messiah as prophesied in the Bible. Going one step further, he also accurately prophesied his own death and resurrection, so we can trust his own claim to be the Son of God.

Reliability of Ancient Manuscripts Confirms Prophecy

Paul carefully stayed on his side of the staircase as he climbed to the holy room where all scribes met to duplicate the scripture. The rules were strict. As little as the slightest touch of someone on the adjacent "down" staircase would mean a return to the bottom for a new ceremonial cleansing. Paul had completed his lengthy training just nine months ago and was eager to embrace, with a passion, his new profession.

Inside the scribal cave Paul retrieved the master scroll of Isaiah, and the duplicate that he had been working on for three months. Setting things up at the long table, he sat down to write. One letter at a time, Paul copied the scroll from the master to the duplicate, stopping at each letter to confirm it. To Paul it seemed inefficient to constantly check every letter since he had memorized the Scripture long ago, but the teaching of scribes was strict and disciplined. Each letter also had to have a thread's width in

191

between and letters and words had to be written in a specific arrangement.

The name of Yahweh came up and Paul stopped to say a sanctification prayer. Then he paused for a moment wondering if the rumors were true. People had said that there would soon be a Jewish revolt against Rome that was sure to spark a war. The Jews had always seemed to have difficulty with Roman control. Paul sighed. At least he was far away from the city of Jerusalem, in the relative safety of the outpost of Qumran.

PERHAPS THE SINGLE MOST IMPORTANT religious archaeological find ever is the discovery of about 800 scrolls in the caves at Qumran on the northwest shore of the Sea of Galilee. These scrolls were written from about 250 B.C. to about A.D. 65 and were discovered by accident in 1947. Scrolls varied in condition from complete, nearly perfect scrolls, to others that were heavily damaged and broken into thousands of fragments. In addition to many scrolls relevant to the Essene culture, every book of the Old Testament was found at Qumran except Esther. The number of portions of Old Testament books found at Qumran is listed below:[1]

Book (in order of Hebrew canon)	Number of Copies (?=possible fragment)
Genesis	18+3?
Exodus	18
Leviticus	17
Numbers	12
Deuteronomy	31+3?
Joshua	2
Judges	3
1–2 Samuel	4

Book (in order of Hebrew canon)	Number of Copies (?=possible fragment)
1–2 Kings	3
Isaiah	22
Jeremiah	6
Ezekiel	7
Twelve (minor prophets)	10+1?
Psalms	39+2?
Proverbs	2
Job	4
Song of Songs	4
Ruth	4
Lamentations	4
Ecclesiastes	3
Esther	0
Daniel	8+1?
Ezra–Nehemiah	1
1–2 Chronicles	1

The scrolls found at Qumran had been buried deep in caves when the Romans were advancing to crush the Jewish revolt that started in A.D. 66. (Jerusalem and the Temple were totally destroyed in A.D. 70, and Jews were expelled from the city.) The Essenes were a sect of pious Jews who had chosen to live in seclusion from the religious mainstream in Jerusalem. They developed a home at an enclave in the city of Qumran on the northwest side of the Dead Sea. Here they practiced strict adherence to the Jewish religion and engaged in devoted copying of Holy Scripture. Copies of scripture and of important Essene documents were stored in pottery jars and then placed in cave libraries. When news of the advancing Romans was received by the

Essenes, the caves at Qumran were abandoned (A.D. 68) and remained untouched for nearly 1,900 years.

In March 1947 a Bedouin shepherd boy named Muhammad was looking for a lost goat in the hills around Qumran. He tossed a rock into a cave and was surprised to hear the shattering of pottery. Investigating the noise, he entered the dark cave and climbed down to where a number of clay jars were discovered that contained leather scrolls wrapped in linen cloth. Because the scrolls had been so carefully prepared and sealed in the clay jars, they were in excellent condition. In the following years, other caves were found containing additional scrolls, bringing the final number to several hundred, with thousands of fragments that are still being analyzed and pieced together.

The importance of the discovery of the Dead Sea Scrolls cannot be overstated in regard to corroborating the accuracy of the biblical manuscripts. For example, a scroll of Isaiah written in 150 B.C., found in nearly perfect condition, was compared to a Masoretic Hebrew text dated in A.D. 916 and found to be consistent after nearly 1,000 years! In fact, of the 166 *words* in chapter 53 in the scroll of Isaiah, only 17 *letters* show any possible signs of change. And in the case of the letters in question, the changes represent matters of spelling and stylistic changes, such as conjunctions, which would have no bearing whatsoever on the meaning of the text.

The discovery of the Dead Sea Scrolls and the comparison of the text with later copies have verified beyond a shadow of a doubt that the Old Testament has accurately been handed down for centuries. This is of immeasurable importance in evaluating the truth and relevance of Jesus because the Old Testament contains many prophecies about the Messiah, that were precisely fulfilled by Jesus.

The Dead Sea Scrolls, containing the prophecies made hundreds of years before Jesus, were themselves written decades, even centuries before Jesus. Thus we know the prophecies were not written "after the fact." This means we can know conclusively that the prophecies were not contrived. This is essential in evaluating the significance of fulfillment of the prophecies by Jesus. When we analyze the statistical odds of so many prophecies coming true in any one man, we find it to be virtually impossible except for divine intervention (see pages 188-89). This leads us to the obvious and important conclusion that Jesus was the Messiah prophesied of in the Old Testament.

Reasons for Scriptural Reliability

When the reliability of the ancient Holy Scripture of the Jews is questioned, it's often because we place it in the context of hand-copying a simple document in the twenty-first century. Certainly today, we would expect errors to be made every time a document is hand-copied. We would naturally expect a document several centuries down the road to bear little resemblance to the original.

However, there are several fundamental differences between hand-copying a document today versus doing the same at the time of Moses. Perhaps most importantly is the state of mind of the Jewish nation, which was a theocracy—a state governed by God. As a theocracy, the holy writings—especially the Law of Moses (the first five books of the Bible)—would be treated with the utmost respect and care. Copies would be closely monitored in the copying process and checked carefully for accuracy. We must also keep in mind that the laws of Moses did not only govern religious activities, but also the judicial activities as well, so accurate copying was crucial.

The practices and ceremonies surrounding the copying of Holy Scripture demonstrated the importance attached to it. First, scribes trained for years to prepare for the important task of copying scripture. They could not practice the profession until age 30. Second, a ceremonial washing was required prior to the copying of any scripture. Third, in certain copyist locations, there were two staircases—one for up and one for down. If a scribe going up into the copy location touched a scribe coming down, he was regarded as "unclean" and had to return to another ceremonial washing before he proceeded.

The name of God was also regarded with enormous reverence. The scribes, fearful of using the Lord God's name in vain (the third commandment) would write the name of God with the middle letters missing (YHWH was written as Y__H). So important was the name of God, that whenever it was about to be written, scribes would say a "sanctification prayer."

The holy scrolls were themselves regarded with extreme reverence. At the end of the useful life of the master scrolls, they were given a ceremonial burial.

Scriptural Copy Rules

The scribes were required to adhere to very precise rules along with a discipline that was ingrained in them during their years of training. The many rules that started with Old Testament scribes included:

1. A synagogue roll must be written on the skins of clean animals, [and]

2. prepared for the particular use of the synagogue by a Jew.

3. These must be fastened together with strings taken from clean animals.

4. Every skin must contain a certain number of columns, equal throughout the entire codex.

5. The length of each column must not extend over less than 48 or more than 60 lines; and the breadth must consist of thirty letters.

6. The whole copy must be first-lined; and if three words be written without a line, it is worthless.

7. The ink should be black, neither red, green, nor any other colour, and be prepared according to a definite recipe.

8. An authentic copy must be the exemplar, from which the transcriber ought not in the least deviate.

9. No word or letter, not even a yod, must be written from memory, the scribe not having looked at the codex before him…

10. Between every consonant the space of a hair or thread must intervene;

11. between every new parashah, or section, the breadth of nine consonants;

12. between every book, three lines.

13. The fifth book of Moses must terminate exactly with a line; but the rest need not do so.

14. Besides this, the copyist must sit in full Jewish dress,

15. wash his whole body,

16. not begin to write the name of God with a pen newly dipped in ink,

17. and should a king address him while writing that name he must take no notice of him.[2]

Apart from these special requirements were the basic scribal rules. The word *scribes* literally means "counters." To verify the accuracy of every scroll that was copied, they had several items that were counted. They counted every letter and compared it to the master scroll. They counted the number of words. And as a final cross-check, they would count through each scroll to the halfway point and compare the letter with the "halfway letter" of the master scroll.

The precision of the Old Testament scribes and the New Testament "professional" copyists was enormous. It is far different than we might expect in today's world.

Memorization of Scripture Increases Reliability

Imagine attempting to alter history, and to alter the words of Holy Scripture. Succeeding would require changing a high percentage of all written scripture to assure that contradictions didn't exist. We know from the Dead Sea Scrolls that that did not happen.

However if someone had really wanted to change Holy Scripture, changing all the written scrolls would not have been enough. Jews in biblical times, especially males, memorized vast amounts of scripture. It was a vital part of their education. If someone wanted to change scripture for some ulterior motive, they would have had to not only change the many copies, but change the memories of many Jews as well. This was certainly not likely in a theocracy where the very words of God were taken so seriously.

The Septuagint

It didn't take long after the conquest of Palestine by Alexander the Great in 331 B.C. before the people in Judea forgot the native language of Hebrew in favor of Koine Greek. When this happened only scribes and a select group of other educated people had the capability to read Holy Scripture. Recognizing this problem, the Jews appointed a group of 70 elders (hence the name Septuagint) to translate the Old Testament into Greek sometime prior to 200 B.C.

The Septuagint was the scripture in common usage at the time of Jesus. Most of the quotations of the Old Testament in the New Testament are from the Septuagint. It would have been the scripture that Jesus used to minister to the common person. In fact, Christians adopted the Septuagint so wholeheartedly that the Jews ultimately lost interest in it and regarded it to be the "Christian Old Testament." Even today, it is regarded as the "official Old Testament" version by the Greek Orthodox Church. Today we have fragments of the Septuagint that date back to before 200 B.C. Some fragments of the Septuagint were found among the Dead Sea Scrolls (the majority of the Dead Sea Scrolls were in Hebrew). There are several reasons why the Septuagint translation is especially important:

1. As mentioned, it was the Old Testament version used by Jesus and, therefore, commands special consideration.

2. Like the Dead Sea Scrolls, the Septuagint establishes the prophecies about Jesus at a point in time *predating* Jesus. We can be certain that the prophecies were not contrived.

3. The Septuagint was translated from Hebrew scripture concurrent or slightly earlier than the earliest existing Hebrew scripture we have today (the Dead Sea Scrolls). Consequently it is useful for clarifying any points of contention.

CONCLUSION

The Dead Sea Scrolls, the Septuagint, the fact that Israel was a theocracy, and the vast memorization of scripture all add up to the enormous reliability of Holy Scripture—both the New Testament and the Old Testament. This is extremely important in regard to the Old Testament because it assures us that the prophecies of Jesus were genuine and made centuries before his birth. This fact allows us to confidently know that he was the prophesied Messiah.

People's Changed Lives Confirm Jesus

As shown throughout this book, there are overwhelming reasons why we can believe what the Bible says about Jesus. Everything we have discussed has dealt with evidence from the past. Is there other evidence? Is there evidence that Jesus is still alive and well today in the hearts of people who feel his presence?

SLOWLY DWAYNE PUSHED ASIDE THE DAMP CARDBOARD that served as his blanket. It had been a long, cold night. He cringed as he swatted his neck in an attempt to kill a roach that had been his bedfellow all night long. The dawn was breaking over the skyscraper-like dumpsters towering over him. A rat scurried across the alley in search of breakfast.

Still groggy from the early morning hour, Dwayne was alert enough to feel the pain of another day. The empty vodka bottle by his side revealed the reason for his headache and the foul taste in his mouth.

Years of alcohol and drug use had led Dwayne through the legal system's revolving door. Fights. Theft. Driving under the influence. He had been in every form of trouble related to addictions. Time after time, his family had bailed him out and covered the many mistakes he'd made. When Dwayne was caught stealing from his mom and dad and later picked up in a drug raid at his brother's home he was told to not come back until he'd straightened his life out.

Dwayne spent the next two years in prison, where he experienced the horrors of inmate brutality. Out of necessity, he learned to fight well. He also learned how to commit burglaries and live on the streets. When he was released on parole, he started manufacturing drugs to make money. Eventually he was caught and returned to prison to finish out his sentence.

Now he was out again. He'd spent the little money he had on vodka to numb the pain before he fell into his bed by the dumpster. It was morning and time to start his new life—again.

After stumbling to his feet, Dwayne staggered down the sidewalk of the ghetto-like town alley. What would he do now? There were not enough people around to panhandle. How would he get money for food? Jumbled thoughts went through his mind as he wandered aimlessly until he reached the steps of a small church. He sat down and placed his head in his hands. He was sick from the night of drunkenness and the despair of facing another wasted phase of life. He started to cry.

A hand softly touched the back of his dirty neck. A kind, burly man named Tom sat beside him and asked him what was wrong. Dwayne, overwhelmed with sadness, told Tom his story. After over an hour of conversation, Tom asked Dwayne if he ever had the chance to learn about Jesus. Dwayne said he attended a church session in prison but didn't get much out of it. Tom invited Dwayne to his home to clean up and to get a hot meal.

After Dwayne showered and ate, Tom explained who Jesus was and why he offered hope to everyone. Tom talked about forgiveness and how God's grace is unlimited. Later that evening they went to church together, and after a few phone calls, Tom found Dwayne a place to stay. As the next few weeks passed, Dwayne was touched by the kindness of the people at Tom's church. He worked at odd jobs and for the first time in years, earned an honest wage. He continued to learn about Jesus and God's unlimited love. Six weeks after his prison release, Dwayne broke down in tears and asked God for forgiveness. He gave his heart and life to Jesus.

Since that time, Dwayne has grown in the faith. He's a frequent participant in activities of the small church that received him so graciously. Starting as a retail clerk, he worked his way up to become the manager of a local hardware store. For the first time, Dwayne is looking ahead with hope. He's contemplating starting a ministry to help others recover from alcohol and drugs.

ASHLEY'S PARENTS DIVORCED WHEN SHE WAS YOUNG. She lived with her father, who molested her when she was five. Although the sexual abuse didn't continue, her father had a parade of ladies who were constantly in and out of the house. Many of them were mean to Ashley, who was "always in the way."

When Ashley turned twelve, boys started to notice her. She was introduced to the world of drugs. Due to the drugs and boys, Ashley convinced herself that she was "happy" and popular. She felt loved by the many boys she was with. At age fifteen, Ashley left her home and her father who had regarded her with such disdain. At first she moved in with a twenty-one-year-old man who lived in a rundown tenement building. But eventually he got tired of Ashley and started seeing other women. Forced to move out, Ashley turned to prostitution to pay for a place to live, food, and money to support her ever-growing drug habit.

Four times Ashley was thrown into jail. The local police knew her as a prostitute and drug user, so every time she was released, it was only a matter of time before she was arrested again.

During one jail stay, Ashley shared a cell with a rather unusual lady—someone unlike the hard core people she usually encountered. This person seemed totally out of place. Doris was highly educated and friendly. She had a good job and a stable living environment. Despite being in jail, Doris was at peace. She read the Bible almost constantly. Ashley noticed how different Doris was and wanted to know more.

Doris had been convicted of shoplifting in a swanky department store during the Christmas season. It had been a horrible year for her financially, and she desperately wanted to get her dying mother a nice gift. So she stole an expensive leather jacket. Doris was convicted and sentenced to spend two weeks in jail. She knew stealing was wrong and regretted her impulsive action. She sincerely confessed her sins to her Lord and Savior, Jesus. She knew that because of her relationship with Him, she would be forgiven even though she had to suffer the consequences of her actions.

Doris was at ease in talking to Ashley. She listened to Ashley's pain in discussing her childhood memories and her subsequent fall into drugs and prostitution. Ashley asked Doris how she remained at such peace in spite of living in a jail cell—a place that was obviously not typical for Doris. Doris then told her about Jesus and the forgiveness and love that he grants everyone.

During the final four days of Doris' stay, Doris and Ashley read the Bible together and prayed together. After two days, Ashley accepted Jesus as her Lord and Savior and decided to start life over again with this new direction. Despite being in jail, she had a new sense of joy and felt able to overcome her problems. Doris invited Ashley to join her at church when she was released.

The day after Ashley got out of jail, she called Doris who was quick to pick her up. The two decided to share an apartment, and Ashley got a job as a waitress at a nearby restaurant.

Although she still deals with the residue of her hard life, Ashley continues to learn from Doris' example as the two read the Bible on a daily basis and attended church regularly. At first Ashley had a difficult time dealing with men at all. She couldn't even have conversations with them. But as she has matured in her faith, even that is changing. Through God's abundant grace, she hopes to someday meet a wonderful man and raise a family. Her new life in Christ has brought her joy and peace—and the promise of a positive future.

BRAD, A WELL-KNOWN ARCHITECT, seemed to have it all. His career had been skyrocketing for years, and he earned a substantial income. He lived in a suburb in a beautiful, four-bedroom house with a pool. He and his wife, Maria, had three children. They owned two luxury automobiles and took at least one vacation a year to some exotic location. They even owned a condominium right by the slopes of a major ski resort. Many of their neighbors were envious.

But inside Brad felt like he was dying. He had no purpose in life and wondered what he had been put on earth for in the first place. These feelings caused him to pour his energy into succeeding at work, acquiring possessions, and entertaining business associates at his condo. While such a focus served him well in his career success, it caused an increasing strain on his marriage, which became secondary to many other interests. In fact, his marriage was falling apart.

One day Brad came home from a business trip and his wife
and three children were gone. Upon his bed was a note which
read:

> Brad, I'm sorry to do this to you, but I just had to
> get away. Our marriage has grown cold. I never see you
> anymore and I can't remember the last time you held
> me in your arms. It seems all I do is care for the children
> as a single parent. Your only use for me seems to be as a
> trophy-wife to use at your business functions. I need
> some time alone to think about things and my future.
> Maria.

Brad was stunned. What had he done? Had he lost his wife
and children? After doing some checking he discovered that
Maria had gone to live with her mother. Despite many calls, he
couldn't get her to talk with him. Brad wondered if everything
from their 15-year marriage was lost. He realized he really loved
his wife, and he had been taking her for granted as he struggled
with his own inner discontent. Now he began to wonder if life
was worth living at all. For the first time ever, he seriously considered suicide.

Brad decided to pack his car with ski gear and go to the condo
early Sunday morning. On the way, he heard an advertisement
for a new church in town. The ad said that everyone has a unique
purpose on earth defined by God. It encouraged people to come
to the morning service to find out more. Brad decided to delay
his trip a couple of hours and find out more.

At church a pastor known for his powerful presentations discussed God's plan for humanity with each person having a specific purpose. He discussed how anyone could know that purpose
and "tap into it" by having a relationship with Jesus and seeking
daily guidance from him. According to the pastor, the steps were
simple and free. At the end of the message, he led the congregation

in a prayer to have a relationship with Jesus and to start on this exciting new journey. Brad accepted the invitation since he had nothing to lose. After the service, he was greeted by several friendly people who discussed what his decision meant and what the next steps were. Instead of going to his condo, Brad spent the entire day at the church getting to know new people. He had a chance to discuss his problem marriage and his feeling of lack of purpose. The church members encouraged him and prayed with him.

Over the next few months, Brad continued to attend the church and participate in a special group for people with marriage problems. The group prayed for their spouses and for guidance. Brad was still not in contact with his wife.

One day Brad came home from a busy day at work, and he saw something strangely familiar. It was his wife's car in the driveway. Breathless with anticipation, he rushed inside to see what was happening. Had she come home to take the rest of her things and ask for a divorce? Or was she back, wanting to work on their marriage? Inside, he was greeted by three joyous children who ran up and jumped into his arms.

"We missed you, Daddy," they said almost in unison.

Then from around the corner came his wife. She looked radiant—more beautiful than on her wedding day.

"I couldn't bear to be without you," Maria said. "While I was gone I attended my mother's church and learned about Jesus Christ. With his help I think we can work out our problems. I started praying for you. I realized I needed to return, and I couldn't wait to talk to you about Jesus."

Brad smiled knowing he had reached the same conclusions. Healing their marriage wasn't going to be easy—but Jesus would give Maria and him the strength and wisdom to persevere.

THESE STORIES ARE COMPOSITES OF TESTIMONIES from people who have accepted Jesus as their Lord and Savior. Jesus is as alive and active today as he ever was. He heals people's marriages, delivers people from the bondage of addictions, renews people's strength when things seem hopeless, and helps people find strength, purpose, and joy in every day.

CONCLUSION

After 2,000 years, Jesus is still changing people's lives. The evidence is startling and overwhelming: Millions of people gladly testify to the positive, dramatic difference Christ has made in their lives and the strength and hope he gives them every day.

Nineteen

Accepting Jesus: A Decision Based on Evidence

The Bible teaches that Jesus is God's ultimate, loving gift to mankind. He is a gift who can provide anyone willing to accept him with an eternal relationship with the God of the universe. Nobody can earn this gift; it is free for those willing to make Jesus their personal Savior and Lord of their lives. Who would not want such a thing?

Yet some people don't accept this gift so wonderfully provided by God's grace. Why not? Perhaps they believe they don't deserve it. Certainly that's true. Nobody is perfect, and nonperfect people really don't deserve a relationship with a perfectly holy God. That's exactly why Jesus was sent to earth—as a perfect sacrifice to redeem imperfect people to him.

Other people are apathetic. They believe that good people go to heaven and bad people go to hell, and what difference does it make regarding their belief in Jesus? However, that's not what the

Bible teaches. It teaches that human beings are saved by grace alone, and that the only way to achieve God's grace is by accepting his loving gift—his Son—and being "born again" in the Spirit. The Bible makes this point very clearly:

> Jesus declared, "I tell you the truth, no one can see the kingdom of God unless he is born again."
>
> "How can a man be born when he is old?" Nicodemus asked. "Surely he cannot enter a second time into his mother's womb to be born!"
>
> Jesus answered, "I tell you the truth, no one can enter the kingdom of God unless he is born of water and the Spirit. Flesh gives birth to flesh, but the Spirit gives birth to spirit" (John 3:3-6).

> "Just as Moses lifted up the snake in the desert, so the Son of Man must be lifted up, that everyone who believes in him may have eternal life.
>
> "For God so loved the world that he gave his one and only Son, that whoever believes in him shall not perish but have eternal life. For God did not send his Son into the world to condemn the world, but to save the world through him. Whoever believes in him is not condemned, but whoever does not believe stands condemned already because he has not believed in the name of God's one and only Son" (John 3:14-18).

> "The Father loves the Son and has placed everything in his hands. Whoever believes in the Son has eternal life, but whoever rejects the Son will not see life, for God's wrath remains on him" (John 3:35-36).

> [*Note:* To fully understand this passage, we should know that "believing" in Jesus—according to the original language—has a fuller, more complete meaning: "to place one's trust" in Jesus.]

Finally, some people simply don't accept the gift of Jesus because they don't believe it. As has been indicated in this book, nonbelief is not an excuse:

1. The tomb was empty. Period. Nobody can deny it, and nobody could produce a corpse of Jesus even though certainly every attempt would have been made to do so to quiet Christianity forever.

2. There were substantial security measures taken at the tomb to ensure that the body of Jesus was protected and that it wouldn't have been stolen.

3. The disciples saw the risen Jesus and certainly would have known the truth. They immediately became uncharacteristically outspoken and all willingly died rather than renounce Jesus. Certainly they would not die for a lie— what would be the purpose?

4. There were many witnesses to the spectacular, memorable events of Jesus. These events would have been discussed for many generations with a great deal of corroboration of the written record that was widely available at the time of the eyewitnesses.

5. There were several well-known, initially "hostile" witnesses (Constantine, Paul, James, and Jude) who changed their minds from doubting the resurrection of Jesus Christ to eventually suffering for him and even placing their lives on the line in painful martyr deaths.

6. There were countless Christian martyrs who died for the historical event of the resurrection of Jesus Christ. Obviously they very strongly believed in the event.

7. The existence of the church is undeniable and indicates an unbroken chain of belief in the historical event of the

resurrection. Without belief in that one historical event, there would be no Christian church.

8. The early writings of the church fathers, providing corroboration of the Bible and further supporting the beliefs proclaimed in the Bible with early creeds, indicate further evidence of belief in Jesus.

9. The rapid explosion of documentation that survived the most intense effort ever made to eradicate a written work, indicates the extensive belief in the events of the New Testament. Cross-checks of documents assure accuracy of the historical account.

10. The non-Christian evidence in often hostile sources supports many claims of the Bible and indicates the reality of the historicity of Jesus.

11. Archaeological evidence supports many events of the New Testament and provides evidence of the vast belief in the resurrection.

12. Complete changes in thinking—from nonbelief to Christianity—by two of the greatest archaeologists of our time seeking to disprove the Bible lends credibility to the accuracy of historically based Christianity.

13. Many specific prophecies of Jesus that were made in the Old Testament and fulfilled in his life, would be statistically impossible if it were not divinely orchestrated that Jesus was the Son of God—the Messiah.

14. The Dead Sea Scrolls and the Septuagint provide irrefutable evidence that the ancient prophecies of Jesus were not tampered with and in fact are reliable.

15. Changed lives of many people today provide continuing evidence that Jesus still exists and interacts in the lives of individuals.

Evidence clearly indicates that Jesus existed and was who he said he was—the Son of God. Once this is realized, a decision needs to be made: to reject or accept him. To reject him means total separation from God. To accept him means the most fulfilling, complete life on this earth imaginable. It leads to purpose in life and to eternal life with the God of the universe.

How to Have a Relationship with Jesus

Jesus said not all who use his name will enter heaven:

> Not everyone who says to me, "Lord, Lord," will enter the kingdom of heaven, but only he who does the will of my Father who is in heaven. Many will say to me on that day, "Lord, Lord, did we not prophesy in your name, and in your name drive out demons and perform many miracles?" Then I will tell them plainly, "I never knew you. Away from me, you evildoers!" (Matthew 7:21-23).

Jesus was referring to people who think using his name along with rules and rituals is the key to heaven. A relationship with God is not based on rituals and rules. It's based on grace, forgiveness, and on having right standing with him through Jesus Christ. Anyone can have a personal relationship with God by following the following steps and praying a simple, sincere prayer:

B*elieve* that God exists and that he came to earth in the human form of Jesus Christ (John 3:16; Romans 10:9).

A*ccept* God's free forgiveness of sins through the death and resurrection of Jesus Christ (Ephesians 1:7-8; 2:8-10)

Switch to God's plan for your life (1 Peter 1:21-23; Ephesians 2:1-5)

Express desire for Christ to be the director of your life (Matthew 7:21-27; 1 John 4:15)

Prayer for Eternal Life with God

Dear God, I believe you sent your Son, Jesus, to die for my sins so I can be forgiven. I'm sorry for my sins, and I want to live the rest of my life the way you want me to. Please put your Spirit in my life to direct me. Amen.

Next Steps

People who have sincerely taken the previous steps automatically become members of God's family of believers. A new world of freedom and strength is available through prayer and obedience to God's will! You can also build your relationship with God by taking the following steps:

- Find a Bible-based church that you like and attend regularly
- Set aside time each day to pray and read the Bible
- Locate other Christians to spend time with on a regular basis

God's Promises to Believers

For Today

But seek first his kingdom and his righteousness, and all these things [things to satisfy all your needs] will be given to you as well (Matthew 6:33).

For Eternity

Whoever believes in the Son has eternal life, but whoever rejects the Son will not see life, for God's wrath remains on him (John 3:36).

Once we develop an eternal perspective, once we establish a relationship with Jesus Christ, even earth's greatest problems fade in significance.

In Closing

Examining the evidence for Jesus is a wise thing to do to build strong support for our faith. Knowing the facts helps us have assurance that we are following a trustworthy leader and not a false leader like a Jim Jones or other, more seductive deceivers. But in the end the important issue is *not* the knowledge gained in knowing beyond a shadow of a doubt that Jesus was who he claimed to be. The important issue is *what we do with that knowledge.*

It is my prayer that you will use the evidence for Jesus to follow him and to help others follow him by taking the simple, free steps outlined on the preceding pages. The blessings that will follow, both on this earth and throughout eternity, are beyond all imagination.

—Ralph O. Muncaster

Notes

Chapter 2: High Security at the Tomb

1. Josh McDowell, *The Resurrection Factor* (San Bernadino, CA: Here's Life Publishers, Inc., 1989), pp. 56-57.

Chapter 3: The Martyrdom of the Apostles

1. Some material in this chapter is drawn from John Foxe, *The New Foxe's Book of Martyrs* (North Brunswick, NJ: Bridge-Logos Publishers, 1997), pp. 5-10.
2. William Stuart McBirnie, Ph.D., *The Search for the Twelve Apostles* (Wheaton, IL: Living Books, 1973), p. 82.

Chapter 4: The Witnesses of Spectacular Events of Jesus

1. Quoting from Richard J. Bauckham, "All in the Family: Identifying Jesus' Relatives," *Bible Review,* April 2000, html version, from http://www.rockinauburn.com/columns/jesus_siblings.htm.
2. Jack Finegan, *The Archeology of the New Testament* (Princeton, NJ: Princeton University Press, 1992).
3. See http://cbn.org/bibleresources/theology/eusebius/churchhistory/eusebius-b3-33.asp.
4. Flavius Josephus, *The Complete Works of Josephus* (Grand Rapids, MI: Kregel Publications, 1981), p. 423.
5. See http://www.misericordia.edu/users/davies/thomas/two.htm, July 2003.
6. See Eusebius, "Ecclesiastical History," 2.23 and http://www.thenazareneway.com/ossuary_of_james.htm, July 2003.

Chapter 6: The Early Christian Martyrs

1. Brian Moynahan, *The Faith, A History of Christianity* (New York: Doubleday, a division of Random House, Inc., 2002), p. 52.
2. Ibid., p. 14.

Chapter 8: The Church Fathers

1. Bruce M. Metzger, *The Text of the New Testament: Its Transmission, Corruption and Restoration* (New York: Oxford University Press, 1968), p. 86.
2. See http://www.bible-researcher.com/canon3.html, July 2003.

Chapter 9: Evidence from Early Manuscripts

1. Life Application Bible (Wheaton, IL: Tyndale House Publishers, Inc.; Grand Rapids, MI: Zondervan Publishing House, 1991), p. 1722.
2. Lee Strobel, *The Case for Christ* (Grand Rapids, MI: Zondervan Publishing House, 1998), pp. 62-63.
3. Josh McDowell, *The New Evidence That Demands a Verdict* (Nashville: Thomas Nelson Publishers, 1999), p. 38.
4. Strobel, *Case for Christ,* p. 64.
5. Norman L. Geisler and William E. Nix, *A General Introduction to the Bible,* 1968 reprint (Chicago: Moody Press, 1980), p. 361.
6. John McRay, *Archaeology and the New Testament* (Grand Rapids, MI: Baker Book House, 1991), p. 356.
7. See http://www.geocities.com/worldview_3/reliabletext.html.

Chapter 10: Evidence from Non-Christian Sources

1. See http://www.facingthechallenge.org/talmud.htm, July 2003.
2. See http://members.aol.com/FLJOSEPHUS/life.htm, maintained by independent scholar G.J. Goldberg, July 2003.
3. See http://www.uncc.edu/jdtabor/josephus-jesus.html, July 2003.
4. See http://www.tektonics.org/tekton_01_01_01_TC.html, July 2003.
5. See http://library.thinkquest.org/11402/bio_pliny_young.html.
6. See www.pbs.org/wgbh/pages/frontline/shows/religion/maps/primary/pliny.html, July 2003. Brackets in original.
7. Suetonius' *Life of the Emperor Claudius,* chapter 25 (excerpt) from http://www.bible-history.com/nero/NEROSuetonius_on_the_Christians.htm, July 2003.
8. Ibid.
9. See http://www.christianstudycenter.com/refs/bios/phlegorphil.htm, July 2003.
10. See http://www.neverthirsty.org/pp/hist/phlegon.html, July 2003.
11. Ibid.
12. Lucian, "The Death of Peregrine," 11-13, in *The Works of Lucian of Samosata,* trans. H.W. Dowler and F.G. Fowler, 4 vols. (Oxford: Clarendon, 1949), vol. 4, cited in Habermas, *The Historical Jesus,* p. 206.
13. See http://members.aol.com/acoxon1274/Hadrian.html, July 2003.

Chapter 11: Archaeological Sites of Jesus

1. Jack Finegan, *The Archeology of the New Testament* (Princeton, NJ: Princeton University Press, 1992), pp. 49-53.
2. Eusebius, *Life of Constantine* 3:41, as referenced by John McRay, *Archaeology and the New Testament* (Grand Rapids, MI: Baker Book House, 1991), p. 156.
3. Ibid., pp. 165-66.
4. See Eusebius, *The Life of Constantine,* book 3, ch. 26.
5. See http://www.us-israel.org/jsource/Archaeology/church.html, July 2003.
6. See http://www.israelmagictours.com/English/ascension_church.htm.

Chapter 12: Other Archaeological Support for Jesus

1. Bible History, www.bible-history.com/pontius_pilate/pilateArchaeology.htm, July 2003.
2. F.F. Bruce, "Archaeological Confirmation of the New Testament," in *Revelation and the Bible,* ed. Carl Henry (Grand Rapids, MI: Baker Book House, 1969), pp. 327-328, as cited by Josh McDowell, *The New Evidence That Demands a Verdict* (Nashville: Thomas Nelson Publisher, 1999), p. 66.

Chapter 13: Great Archaeologists Convert to Christianity

1. William Foxwell Albright to John C. Trevor (March 1948) from http://religion.rutgers.edu/iho/dss.html.
2. See http://www.bible-history.com/quotes/william_f_albright_3.html, July 2003.
3. Dr. Norman Geisler, the Till–Geisler debate from http://www.angelfire.com/co/jesusFreak/resourses.html.

Chapter 14: Miraculous Prophecy Forecasts Jesus' Life and Ministry

1. See http://www.census.gov/ipc/www/worldhis.html, July 2003.
2. Flavius Josephus, "Antiquities of the Jews," chapter VIII, sections 1–5, trans. William Whiston, *The Complete Works of Josephus* (Grand Rapids, MI: Kregel Publications, 1981), p. 375.

Chapter 15: Prophecies Leading Up to Jesus' Crucifixion

1. Harold Hoehner, *Chronological Aspects of the Life of Christ* (Grand Rapids, MI: Zondervan Publishing House, 1977), p. 131.
2. Ibid., p. 138.

Chapter 17: Reliability of Ancient Manuscripts Confirms Prophecy

1. Josh McDowell, *The New Evidence That Demands a Verdict* (Nashville: Thomas Nelson Publisher, 1999), p. 80.
2. Samuel Davidson, "The Hebrew Text of the Old Testament," London: 1856, p. 89, quoted in Norman L. Geisler and William E. Nix, *General Introduction to the Bible* (Chicago: Moody Press, 1986).

Other Books by
Ralph O. Muncaster

A Skeptic's Search for God

Dismantling Evolution

Examine the Evidence® Series

Can You Trust the Bible?

Creation vs. Evolution

Creation vs. Evolution DVD

How to Talk About Jesus With the Skeptics in Your Life

Science—Was the Bible Ahead of Its Time?

What Is the Trinity?

What Really Happens When You Die?

Why Are Scientists Turning to God?

Why Does God Allow Suffering?